Facilitating Researchers in
Insecure Zones

Facilitating Researchers in Insecure Zones

Towards a More Equitable Knowledge Production

Edited by Oscar Abedi Dunia,
Anju Oseema Maria Toppo and
James B.M. Vincent

BLOOMSBURY ACADEMIC
LONDON • NEW YORK • OXFORD • NEW DELHI • SYDNEY

BLOOMSBURY ACADEMIC
Bloomsbury Publishing Plc
50 Bedford Square, London, WC1B 3DP, UK
1385 Broadway, New York, NY 10018, USA
29 Earlsfort Terrace, Dublin 2, Ireland

BLOOMSBURY, BLOOMSBURY ACADEMIC and the Diana logo
are trademarks of Bloomsbury Publishing Plc

First published in Great Britain 2023

Copyright © Oscar Abedi Dunia, Anju Oseema Maria Toppo and James B.M. Vincent and Contributors, 2023

Oscar Abedi Dunia, Anju Oseema Maria Toppo and James B.M. Vincent have asserted their right under the Copyright, Designs and Patents Act, 1988, to be identified as Editors of this work.

Cover design by Charlotte James
Cover image © CSA-Printstock/ Getty Images

All rights reserved. No part of this publication may be reproduced or transmitted in any form or by any means, electronic or mechanical, including photocopying, recording, or any information storage or retrieval system, without prior permission in writing from the publishers.

Bloomsbury Publishing Plc does not have any control over, or responsibility for, any third-party websites referred to or in this book. All internet addresses given in this book were correct at the time of going to press. The author and publisher regret any inconvenience caused if addresses have changed or sites have ceased to exist, but can accept no responsibility for any such changes.

A catalogue record for this book is available from the British Library.

A catalog record for this book is available from the Library of Congress.

ISBN:	HB:	978-1-3502-6566-0
	PB:	978-1-3502-6565-3
	ePDF:	978-1-3502-6568-4
	eBook:	978-1-3502-6567-7

Typeset by Integra Software Services Pvt. Ltd.

To find out more about our authors and books visit www.bloomsbury.com and sign up for our newsletters.

Contents

List of contributors		vi
1	Introduction: Setting the stage	1
2	Getting and keeping engaged	25
3	The indispensable bridge: Without us no research	51
4	Systematically silenced and non-recognized	71
5	Managing various aspects of insecurity	93
6	Beyond a narrow North/South divide	117
7	Beyond the bleak picture	139
8	The need of change: What, how and who?	157
References		176
Index		183

Contributors

Oscar Abedi Dunia is an independent researcher who is also the president of the NGO Aide Rapide aux victimes des catastrophes et Recherche (ARCV), based in South Kivu, in the DR Congo. He has over fifteen years of experience from working with research on conflict dynamics and armed groups in the eastern DRC. He has been working with research teams and individual researchers from Europe and the United States, as well as the UN mission, various international humanitarian organizations and journalists.

Paul Amara Moiwo is based in the southern Sierra Leonean city Bo. He has worked with several European researchers and students in Sierra Leone on various research themes. He has especially been part of teams working with the dynamics of war. He lived in the occupied city during the war and from contacts there he had a privileged position researching the war with members from both the Revolutionary United Front (RUF) and the Sierra Leone Border guards (RSLAF).

Peter Foday Bangura is an NGO worker who has worked with several researchers from Europe and the United States. Peter has worked with researchers and research teams focusing on thematic areas, including conflict dynamics, gender-based violence and general community-related challenges in Sierra Leone. He is also a graduate from the University of Sierra Leone.

Eric Batumike Banyanga is a teacher in the History Department at the Institut Supérieur Pédagogique in Bukavu, DR Congo. He is also affiliated researcher at the interdisciplinary research group, Le Groupe d'Etudes sur les Conflits et la Sécurité Humaine (GEC-SH) based in Bukavu at the Centre de Recherche Universitaire du Kivu (CERUKI). He has over six years of experience conducting research on various issues such as urban and rural security dynamics, land conflicts, the history of disease and politics in the Congo. He has worked with several research teams and researchers from Europe and the United States.

Stanislas Bisimwa – Baganda is an independent researcher based in South Kivu, DR Congo. He is linked to the interdisciplinary research group, Le Groupe d'Etudes sur les Conflits et la Sécurité Humaine, (GEC-SH). He has over eight years of experience working with research on various issues such as mental health of victims of traumatic events in the city of Bukavu, armed groups and public power (for the Rift Valley Institute/Usalama Project), kidnapping, circular return of armed groups in DR Congo, the political economy of elections, socio-political dynamics of roadblocks, dynamics of conflicts in Eastern DR Congo (in the framework of the ProPaix I and II project), community perceptions of humanitarian actions in Eastern DR Congo as well as migration dynamics in the Great Lakes region. He has worked with research teams and individual researchers from Europe, Africa as well as from United Nations missions and International Organizations and journalists.

Elisée Cirhuza Balolage is a researcher with the interdisciplinary research group, Le Groupe d'Etudes sur les Conflits et la Sécurité Humaine (GEC-SH/ ISP-Bukavu) in D. R. Congo since 2018. His research focuses on the dynamics of land conflicts, street protests in peri-urban cities and tensions in the energy sector. He has conducted research for various European and American research centers as well as international and national Humanitarian Organizations in Eastern DR Congo.

Karin Elfving has a masters in cultural analysis and international journalism. Her masters thesis in international journalism focuses on so-called 'fixers' in journalistic settings. Since 2011, she is part of an initiative seeking to enhance the visibility of journalists in Africa, Asia and Latin America by editing and translating articles written by journalists in these regions which are later published in Swedish media.

For several years Karin was teaching ethnology at Umeå University and Södertörn University in Sweden. She also works as a translator from Swedish, French, Spanish and English.

Maria Eriksson Baaz is Professor in Political Science at the Department of Government, Uppsala University Sweden. Her research spans over gender and war, critical military studies, post-colonial theory and research ethics and she has conducted extensive research in the DR Congo. She has authored several books, such as *The Paternalism of Partnership: A Postcolonial Reading of Identity in Development Aid* (Zed Books, 2005) and *Sexual Violence as a Weapon of War? Perceptions, Prescriptions, Problems in the Congo and Beyond* (Zed Books, 2015, with Maria Stern) and her articles have appeared in several leading international peer-reviewed journals.

Abu Bakarr Jaward is an independent researcher who has supported researchers who have conducted research on armed groups, conflict dynamics and humanitarian security for many years in Sierra Leone. He is a former child soldier and an ex-border guard of the Republic Sierra Leone Armed forces (RSLAF). He is presently resident in Freetown and working at the Sierra Leone ports Authority.

Lansana Juana is an independent research assistant, presently working with the Ministry of Basic and Secondary Education in Sierra Leone. He has an MPhil degree in Gender and Development from the University of Sierra Leone. He has been in research for the last twenty-two years supporting visiting researchers from Europe. He has undertaken research in the areas such as conflict resolution, children and youth affected by wars, early and forced marriages, sexual and gender-based violence, just to name a few.

John Ferekani Lulindi is an independent researcher and public health expert based in South Kivu, the DR Congo. He has several years of research experience with research teams from various countries addressing, in particular, issues around food security, health and nutrition and sexual and gender-based violence. He also has much professional experience in monitoring and evaluation of emergency and development projects in these areas.

Pascal Kizee Imili is an independent researcher since June 2016 and a member of the Centre Indépendant et de Recherches Stratégiques au Kivu (CIRESKI), based in Uvira in South Kivu. He has conducted research together with researchers from European universities and international and national NGOs, on a range of topics such as the exploitation of children as laborers in the mining areas, conflicts between herders and farmers, the socio-economic integration between the local population and the military and their dependents in post-conflict areas, to name but a few.

Evariste Mahamba is a journalist, writer, researcher and expert-trainer in communication aiming to bring about behaviour change. He has conducted research and written several articles on development, security and conflict, particularly related to protected areas and natural and natural resource exploitation in eastern DRC. He has also conducted several trainings on journalism and community radio management and marketing of community radio stations.

Jérémie Mapatano is an independent researcher affiliated researcher at the interdisciplinary research group Le Groupe d'Etudes sur les Conflits et la Sécurité Humaine (GEC-SH) based in Bukavu, the DR Congo. He has several years of experience of research on conflict and humanitarian issues, working with individual researchers as well as research teams from Europe and the United States. Recently he is also involved in child protection activities for the International Rescue Committee/IRC in DRC.

Francine Mudunga is a research assistant at the interdisciplinary research group, Le Groupe d'Etudes sur les Conflits et la Sécurité

Humaine (GEC-SH) based in Bukavu. She has five years of research experience, working with different researchers and research teams, on issues around urban security and land governance. Her research interests are in rural sociology with a focus on peasant dynamics and rural development.

Bienvenu Mukungilwa is a Research Assistant at the Institut Supérieur Pédagogique de Bukavu (ISP-Bukavu) and a researcher affiliated with the interdisciplinary research group, Le Groupe d'Etudes sur les Conflits et la Sécurité Humaine (GEC-SH) based in Bukavu since 2017. He recently embarked upon a PhD programme in Cultural Anthropology at the University of Florida in the United States.

Lebon Mulimbi is an independent researcher and analyst on conflict dynamics since 2003. He is also the National Coordinator of 'l' Action pour la Protection des Droits Humains et de Développement Communautaire' (APDHUD). He has participated in several research projects involving European, American, Asian and African universities, in different fields, such as studies on armed groups, land conflicts, customary power conflicts, governance and democracy, justice and security, taxation, barrier politics, gender, child protection, mining conflict and analysis of the socio-political, security and judicial context. Through this work he has facilitated a number of research projects, PhD and Masters projects, as well as UN and other expert group reports.

Aisha Kamara has an MPhil in Rural Development from the Fourah Bay College (University of Sierra Leone). She is a senior researcher with a focus on women and children's rights and well-being. She has been the national coordinator of SLANGO, the main umbrella organization for NGOs in the country. As an independent researcher she has over the last few years focused on socio-economic aspects of mining in rural communities.

Yusuf Kamara is an independent researcher, with a master's degree in Peace and Development from Njala University, Sierra Leone. He is also a manager for monitoring, evaluation and learning at the National Youth Commission (NAYCOM). He has worked extensively with overseas researchers, with both policy and academic backgrounds. He has chiefly worked on projects related to youth empowerment and employment creation, but has extensive experience of research in peace and conflict prevention, and has also worked on the theme of sexual and gender-based violence.

Ahmadu Kanneh is a graduate from Fourah Bay College in Freetown. He is a Sierra Leone police officer at the medium level. He has worked as a research assistant in Sierra Leone for over sixteen years. He also undertakes independent research and is presently pursuing a Law degree in Russia federation.

Hakeem Mansaray has a Bachelors degree from Njala University, in Sierra Leone, and is currently employed as a teacher at the SOS children's Villages in Sierra Leone. He was previously working as a facilitating researcher for a couple of years teaming up with researchers from Europe.

Lievin Mbarushimana-Mukingi is an independent researcher who has conducted research on armed groups, conflict dynamics and humanitarian security for many tears. He also worked as an assistant to the UN expert groups on the DRC from 2011 to 2019. He has conducted research on behalf of several European universities, especially on issues around armed groups in North and South Kivu and Ituri and conflicts related to customary law and land.

Anju Oseema Maria Toppo is an Assistant Professor at the Department of History, St. Xavier's College, Ranchi in Jharkhand, India. She has served as guest faculty at Nirmala College and at the PG Department of History, Ranchi University. Her ongoing research is on gender and forest management, focused on the empowerment of indigenous women in Jharkhand. She is also active in the social and resistance movements of the Adivasi (indigenous) population of Jharkhand. She holds a master's degree in History from Loyola College, Chennai and is currently a doctoral researcher, affiliated to Ranchi University.

Swati Parashar is Professor in Peace and Development at the School of Global Studies, Gothenburg University, Sweden. She is the author of *Women and Militant Wars: The Politics of Injury* (Routledge, 2014) and has published several journal articles, book chapters and popular media pieces. She is the co-editor of the *Routledge Handbook of Feminist Peace Research* (2021) with Tarja Väyrynen, Élise Féron and Catia Cecilia Confortini; *Rethinking Silence, Voice and Agency in Contested Gendered Terrains* (Routledge, 2019) with Jane Parpart; and *Revisiting Gendered States: Feminist Imaginings of the State in International Relations* (OUP, 2018) with J. Ann Tickner and Jacqui True. She is a co-editor in chief of the *International Feminist Journal of Politics* and serves on the advisory boards of several journals.

Darwin Rakanyaga Assuamani is an independent researcher based in South Kivu, DR Congo. Since 2008, he is the national coordinator of a Congolese rights organization called ARVC (Aide rapide aux victimes des catastrophes). He has thirteen years of experience in research and interventions on various themes such as conflict dynamics, early and forced marriages, sexual and gender-based violence. He has also participated in various trainings on gender, humanitarian action and community behaviour change with UNOCHA, INEE in Dakar Senegal and Côte d'Ivoire.

Anita Marion Rogers is a registered nurse and is presently working for an International Hospital in Sierra Leone. As a facilitating researcher she has mainly been part of larger teams doing quantitative studies. Within the medical fields she has worked with researchers from Europe and the United States.

Alie Sesay holds a degree in accounting with certificates from the UK and has over twenty years' experience of facilitating research. He has been part of all sorts of research teams and has a wealth of experience working on various thematic areas in governance, peace building, conflict resolution and community-related activities. He has worked with various researchers from across the world.

James B.M. Vincent holds a Master of Arts degree in Governance and development from the Institute of Development Studies, University of Sussex, UK, and is a researcher and consultant on Governance, Development and Conflict-related issues, on Youth issues especially youth development and employment creation programmes and Agriculture in Sierra Leone and the Mano River region. He is the author of *A Village-Up View of Sierra Leone's Civil War and Reconstruction: Multi-layered and Networked Governance*, and has co-authored a number of chapters in books.

Mats Utas is professor in Cultural Anthropology at Uppsala University. His research and scholarship have mainly focused on conflict and post-conflict situations with a particular focus on West Africa. Utas is the editor of *African Conflicts and Informal Power: Big Men and networks* (Zed Books, 2012) and co-editor (with Paul Higate) of *Private Security in Africa: From the Global Assemblage to the Everyday* (Zed Books, 2017). In addition to these, Utas has published articles and chapters in leading journals and edited book volumes.

In memory of
Tamba Lebbie 1976–2021

1

Introduction: Setting the stage

Oscar Abedi Dunia, Maria Eriksson Baaz, Swati Parashar, Anju Oseema Maria Toppo, Mats Utas, James B.M. Vincent and Karin Elfving

Research here in the DRC is like the coltan and other minerals. Other countries that don't have access to it claim it and benefit from it. It is the same with research. The research would not be possible without us. Still, it is people from the outside who profit from it, get visibility, funding and are called experts. At the same time, we – the ones who provide access, adapt the methodology and questions and collect the data in very precarious circumstances – get little compensation and are not acknowledged. It is sort of a continuation of colonial relations.
(Participant eastern DR Congo workshop)

The (contracting) researchers act as if they are very knowledgeable to which I disagree. Because any person who has intellect will do something for displaced, will do something for Adivasi men and women fighting police atrocities. They can help us in cases, can suggest us means for redressal, can provide help of NGOs. But only when they need us to work for them they assure us help, but once the fieldwork is over they never keep their word. They not only use us but also the people through us.
(Interview Jharkhand/India)

Delaying or not signing a contract which happens a lot, that's a way of exploiting. Because if you go into the field without signing, you will not know. There can be things in the ToR that you don't have

in mind because you haven't seen it yet. So, then they can benefit and afterwards they give you the contract to sign. I think that is exploitation .... But how I see it, you must care for people first. You can't just go and take something from them. If something goes wrong, this is most likely the reason. If I don't like you, I can start to distort information. It doesn't need to be intentional, but I will make less effort.

(Participant Sierra Leone workshop)

The voices above capture some of the experiences of a group of professionals whom we, in this book, will call 'facilitating researchers'. We define a 'facilitating researcher' as a key agent, based in the research setting, who performs research but who also regulates the access and flow of knowledge between 'contracting researchers' and the researched. By contracting researchers, we refer to researchers with access to research funding who contract other researchers, often based in the data-collection/research setting, to conduct research tasks. We will explain and motivate these concepts further in this introduction.

In this book facilitating researchers in three settings, currently or previously afflicted by armed conflict – namely the eastern Democratic Republic of the Congo (DRC), Sierra Leone and Jharkhand in India – account for our/their experiences. As reflected in the citations, most of the facilitating researchers' experiences revolve around unequal relations and, at times, even sentiments of exploitation. There is (most often) a marked inequality between facilitating researchers and 'contracting researchers'. While facilitating researchers play a crucial role in the research process, we/they seldom get proper, if any, credit for it.

In this book facilitating researchers recount the various and crucial roles that we/they occupy in the field and how we/they still most often are systematically erased and made invisible in the final research texts. The book bears witness to the often-marked inequalities between facilitating researchers and 'contracting researchers', in particular, but not only, 'contracting researchers' based in the Global North. The authors recount how facilitating researchers often navigate insecurities with scarce resources on behalf of others. Yet, the book goes beyond simply accounting for experiences of unequal relationships. We, by describing lived experiences and by proposing concrete institutional changes, highlight the possibility of working in a different manner. At the end of the book we outline various routes forward to make fieldwork and research a non-exploitative experience in collaborative knowledge production and community building.

While the focus of the book is on facilitating-contracting research relations in insecure settings, affected or previously affected by armed conflict, we believe that it is relevant for researchers engaged in North-South knowledge production more generally. The various forms of insecurities in livelihoods, remuneration and access to basic security accounted for are clearly not unique to facilitating researchers in conflict and post-conflict settings. Neither are insecurities in the form of risks related to violence and incarceration. Such risks are present in any settings in which research topics are perceived as sensitive or threatening. In addition, by addressing power inequalities in research and, in the conclusion chapter also situating these in the context of academic cultures and practices more generally, we believe that the book may also be relevant for researchers who engage in research collaborations more generally, beyond North-South divides.

Research on and debates on inequalities in North-South knowledge production go long back, involving numerous commentators and scholars – some of whom we will mention in the overview later in this introduction. Yet, the general debate on inequalities in North-South knowledge production tends to focus on more established scholars in the Global South who hold permanent positions, a PhD degree or more (Collyer 2018). While such a focus in part can be seen as warranted, it tends to neglect that many engaged in research in the Global South do not hold PhDs, in part as the possibilities and resources to complete a PhD in many settings are exceedingly limited. Many who engage in research collaboration with contracting researchers remain in more or less insecure teaching positions at universities without a PhD during their entire career. Others are not formally connected to a university but are self-employed. Yet, they have substantial research experience through their engagement with academic researchers as well as international and national organizations. Hence, facilitating researchers as defined here constitute an essential and large group in many countries in the Global South, which is often neglected in debates on inequalities in knowledge production across North and South.

'Us/They?': The background of this book

The reader of this chapter has probably already started to wonder what the somewhat awkward 'us/they' refer to and is doing in the text. So, let us start with explaining this, and thereby provide a background to the book.

The 'us/they' here refers to the fact that the authors of this chapter as well as the concluding chapter are both 'facilitating researchers' and 'contracting researchers'. Ideally this book would not require an 'us/they': the research funding should have gone straight to the editors of this book/the facilitating researchers and the book should have been written in a truer 'we-form' (even if there clearly is no homogeneous facilitating research experience). Yet, instead the book is an outcome of, and reflects the very processes, structures and relations that it problematizes and seeks to challenge.

The book is an outcome of a research project funded by research grants only available for Sweden-based researchers as lead applicants. Hence, it reflects the unequal funding structure for research in which large part of research funding tends to be available only for researchers in the Global North, creating problematic and systemic power inequalities (c.f. Erondu et al. 2021). Moreover, although clearly inspired by various conversations with facilitating researchers in the field – not the least Abedi Dunia, Oseema Maria Toppo and Vincent – the project idea and proposal were conceived by the three Northern-based contracting researchers/authors Eriksson Baaz, Parashar and Utas.[1] The participatory set-up with workshops joining facilitating researchers in the DR Congo, Sierra Leone and India was outlined in the project proposal. Yet, the particular facilitating researchers and editors of this book – Abedi Dunia, Oseema Toppo and Vincent – were engaged only after the project was granted funding.

Hence, and similar to many other projects, the set-up was not a result of a true collaborative effort, but decided upon by Eriksson Baaz, Parashar and Utas. As such, not only the basic set-up and methodology of the project, but also timelines and, not the least, budget-lines, including salaries were decided by these three privileged Northern-based researchers. Also, this book – written by facilitating researchers – was part of the supposed output of the project, again decided by Eriksson Baaz, Parashar and Utas. Once funding was secured the project largely followed the set-up in the research application. In Sierra Leone and DR Congo, workshops with facilitating researchers were organized and managed by Abedi Dunia and Vincent in 2019. One workshop with fifteen participants was arranged in Sierra Leone, where Utas also participated. In the DR Congo two workshops, joining thirty researchers, were organized by Abedi Dunia and Eriksson Baaz participated in one of those. In India, the Covid pandemic interfered and the planned workshops had to be replaced with interviews and focus groups conducted by Oseema Maria Toppo.

The book is based on the transcripts of the discussions in these workshops as well as the interviews conducted. The main role of Eriksson Baaz, Parashar and Utas has been to co-ordinate the writing process, communicate with the publisher and draft this introduction and the concluding chapter. They/we were given (or perhaps took) that responsibility since they/we, as a result of the wider project that the book forms part of, are more familiar with the wider literature and the workings of various academic institutions and publishers.

---

[1] We would like to thank Judith Verweijen who was part of an earlier version of the research application for providing much valuable inputs and ideas.

We will provide additional information about the writing process by the end of this chapter.

Returning then to the initial question of 'we/they': it reflects the fact that the book and in particular this introduction and the concluding chapter has been written by both facilitating researchers and contracting researchers. Clearly, we could have opted for another route: to write the whole book in a facilitating researcher we-voice. Yet, we think that that would be a dishonest representation, downplaying the fact that the book is an outcome of, and reflects the very inequalities that the book problematizes and seeks to challenge.

In the same vein, Eriksson Baaz, Parashar and Utas would like to point out that they/we do not in any way see ourselves/themselves as different or any better than most other contracting researchers. We/they have, for instance, also failed to provide proper recognition to facilitating researchers, often reducing the contribution to acknowledgement in footnotes, not contemplating co-authorship.

In the remaining part of this introduction chapter, we will first explain the choice of, and meaning we provide to, the term 'facilitating researchers' and 'contracting researchers'. After this we will situate the book in the wider literature and previous research, before we move on to elaborate on some additional methodological and ethical issues.

Facilitating researchers and contracting researchers?

What then do we mean by 'facilitating researchers' and 'contracting researchers', and why did we choose these terms? Let us start with the more uncomplicated concept, that of 'contracting or comissioning researchers'. By this term we simply refer to researchers with access to research funding who contract other researchers, often based in the data-collection/research setting, to conduct research tasks. We avoid the otherwise common terms 'White', 'Western' or even 'Northern-based' researchers as much research today, including research which engages facilitating researchers, is conducted by researchers based in, or originating from, the Global South and who are neither 'White', 'Western' nor based in the Global North. In addition to choosing a neutral concept (i.e. in terms of race/origin), the book also acknowledges and addresses the need to further acknowledge research conducted in the Global South in Chapter 6: *Beyond a narrow South/North divide*. This chapter highlights and demonstrates how marked inequalities and exploitation in research relations also take place within national contexts, sometimes by researchers who themselves have been engaged by a contracting researcher in the Global North and, in turn, sub-contracts parts of the research tasks to other facilitating researchers. In short, while the book mainly reflects experiences of working with 'White', 'Western' or 'Western/Northern-based' researchers, we seek to highlight that inequalities in knowledge production go far beyond North/South divides.

Let us now turn to the more complex notion of 'facilitating researcher'. The concepts otherwise commonly used to describe this role are – various combinations of – 'brokers', 'assistants', 'fixers' or 'local researchers' (de Jong 2018; Dean and Stevano 2016; Eriksson Baaz 2019; Gupta 2014; Jenkins 2015; Käihkö 2019; Malony and Hammett 2007; Parashar 2019; Sangarasivam 2001; Turner 2013; Utas 2019). Yet, as we concluded in the various workshops, all these concepts have some problematic connotations, even though the meanings we attach to them differ between us. The term 'broker' – and clearly to an even greater extent so – the term 'fixer', more often used amongst journalists (Borpujari 2019; Murrell 2015; Palmer 2018, 2019; Plaut and Kelin 2019), carry quite pejorative meanings which also downplay the research conducted by many facilitating researchers.

The possibility to use the commonplace 'local assistants' or 'local researchers' was also discussed, but eventually discarded. The term 'local assistants' was dismissed on the grounds that it downplays the often-crucial role that many facilitating researchers perform to merely 'assistance'. However, another problem with the notion of 'local assistants', also reflected in the concept 'local researchers', is attached to the notion of 'the local'. The problem with the notion of 'local researchers' is that it is provided with meaning through its imagined opposition to – supposedly less local, and somehow more superior and advanced – 'international' or 'expatriate' researchers. As concluded, particularly in the DRC workshops, 'everyone is local' – hence adding to critical debates on the concept of the 'local' (Hirblinger and Simons 2015; c.f. Jabri 2013; Sabaratnam 2013).

Our discussions during the various (yet separate) workshops eventually made us decide on the concept of 'facilitating researchers'. By the notion of 'researchers' we aim to avoid the downplaying of the research contribution that facilitating researchers make. Through the concept 'facilitating' we seek to maintain some of the crucial connotations about 'in between-ness' and 'facilitation' attached to the broader notion of 'broker', while avoiding the negative connotations that the broker concept has particularly in India (see Björkman 2021), as was pointed out by our Indian participants. The notion of 'in between-ness' in facilitation – in combination with the fact that few facilitating researchers enjoy the benefits of working under clear contracts – is the main reason why we opted for 'facilitating', rather than the more neutral term 'contracted'.

In short, we define a 'facilitating researcher' as a key agent performing research tasks who occupies a position in-between contracting researchers and the researched, regulating the access and flow of knowledge between them. This label could be put on many researchers engaged by contracting researchers anywhere. Yet, the focus of this book is on facilitating researchers' experiences *as based in/living in or close to the data-collection/research settings*. This position is quite different from other researchers who may 'occupy a position in-between contracting researchers and the researched, regulating the access and flow of knowledge between them'. Clearly, there are many researchers occupying such roles (such as, for instance, other scholars or students based at various universities in or outside the country of research) who are not living in the context in which the research is conducted.

In contrast to such people, the experiences of facilitating researchers accounted for here are deeply connected to the fact that we/they are based in or at least close to the research settings where we/they work and are contracted to work. This positionality both provides us/them with the very opportunities to act as facilitating researchers due to networks, familiarity with the contexts, embodied cultural and language skills. At the same time, and as we will highlight in the book, it also constitutes a major source of additional work as well as insecurities – which is seldom recognized or remunerated. While contracting researchers experience of tense relations with, or even threats from, various stakeholders in the research setting tend to be limited to the time they spend 'in the field', facilitating researchers are often left to handle such issues and thus live with our/their involvement in research projects for a long time after data collection is completed (see also Grimmm et al. 2020; Jenkins 2015; Mapatano 2019; Middleton and Pradhan 2014; Thamani 2019).

Importantly, and as we will highlight particularly in Chapter 6 the boundaries between facilitating researchers and contracting researchers are sometimes blurred. Or differently put, at times a researcher may take on both the role as a contracting and facilitating researcher, when they/we act as intermediaries between a contracting researcher with access to funding with whom he/she enters a contract but sub-contracts part of the work to other facilitating researchers. Abedi Dunia, Vincent and Oseema Maria Toppo have experience also of this.

Situating the book in other research and debates in the social sciences

We will now move to situating the book in the wider academic literature. Anthropologists have written extensively about the relations in fieldwork, often using terms such as 'assistants', 'informants' or 'interlocutors' for the latter (for early writings in anthropology, see e.g. Griaule 1948; Grindal and Salamone 1995; Powdermaker 1966; Turner

1967). Yet, most of these anthropological accounts have focused on fieldwork practices and lived experiences of researchers in relation to the local people, focusing little on facilitating researchers. Like other disciplines, anthropology has, in large, been based on the idea of the lone researcher as 'a sole vessel of observation and analysis' (Cons 2014: 376) or 'the lone gun' (Bloor et al. 2010). Yet, one can discern a trend towards more methodological reflections around fieldwork, including some works co-published with research 'assistants', such as Middleton and Pradhan (2014), Hoffman and Tarawalley (2014).

International Relations (IR) and Political Science, dominated by quantitative methods, have adopted embedded fieldwork methodologies only in recent times and have thus, (compared to anthropology) lagged behind in terms of debates on research ethics and fieldwork practices. Yet, as conflict research in political science, IR and human geography become more complex and nuanced, research ethics have become the focus of many discussions. The role of research brokers and/or assistants has been addressed in some of these discussions (Bliesemann de Guevara and Bøås 2020; Cronin-Furman and Lake 2018; Hoover Green and Cohen 2021; Themner 2022; Vlassenroot 2006).

In short, there has been an upsurge of interest in questions related to research ethics in the last years, including exploitative practices by contracting researchers. Moreover, and most importantly, the voices of facilitating researchers themselves have been increasingly heard. One example of this, where some of the Congolese authors in this book have contributed, is the Silent Voices blog organized by Ghent University where facilitating/brokering researchers write themselves.[2] Hence, there appears to be a break of the dominant trend in which contracting researchers speak *for* facilitating researchers.

There is reason to believe that questions around sub-contracting and facilitating researchers will become increasingly important. During the recent decade we have already witnessed what is often referred to as an increasing securitization of academic research (Peter and

---

[2] https://www.gicnetwork.be/silent-voices-blog/.

Strazzari 2017). Research institutions in Europe and the United States have increasingly come to regulate and restrict fieldwork access due to security concerns of their own staff. This has led to more so-called 'remote research practices', whereby contracting researchers outsource data collection to facilitating researchers. In short, it has become more common to see contracting researchers remain in the comfort of their country or stay in comfortable hotels in safe urban settings, while facilitating researchers collect data for them/us.

The restrictions attached to the Covid-19 pandemic clearly limited contracting researchers' possibilities to be present 'in the field' even more, in turn further highlighting the role of facilitating researchers (see Abedi Dunia et al. 2023; Mwambari et al. 2021). While restrictions attached to the pandemic are short-term, we anticipate a continuation of restrictions and remote research practices after Covid-19. In fact, it is perhaps something that not only we, but also the readers of this book, should hope for. Decreasing international air travel is one of the crucial measures needed to mitigate the massive and truly global challenges of climate change. The inequalities between the Global North and South in terms of responsibility for climate change and climate action have to be considered here, making limited opportunities to travel be more evenly distributed (c.f. Higham and Font 2020; Nevins et al. 2022).

In short, we face the challenge of increasing long-distance/remote research. Most of the limited literature addressing this highlights how it may increase the risk of exploitative and unequal research relationships and partnerships (Middleton and Pradhan 2014; cf. Sukarieh and Tannock 2019; Turner 2013). Yet, that is not necessarily the case. The increasing outsourcing or 'long-distance approaches' are not necessarily negative. Instead, they may offer new opportunities for facilitating researchers and can lead to more emancipatory ways of co-producing knowledge (Abedi Dunia et al. 2023; Mwambari et al. 2021; Myrttinen and Mastonshoeva 2019; Vogel and Musamba 2022).

In the next section, we will shortly account for some of the debates in the existing literature addressing facilitating researchers (yet, though other concepts), by focusing on two themes that are also central to this book. The first concerns the issue of researcher safety/security, which has received increasing attention in the literature in recent years, and which is also a major concern in this book – albeit in a different manner. The second theme focuses more specifically on North-South knowledge production and what existing literature has to say about the relationship between facilitating researchers (though named differently) and contracting researchers.

Largely invisible in the increasing attention to research security

Lately we have, as alluded to above, witnessed how '[a]dditional resources are put into ensuring the physical safety of (read: contracting) researchers, and into securing data along the research supply-chain' (Peter and Strazzari 2017: 1532). As a manifestation of this increasing securitization of research, there has been an upsurge of attention to researcher safety, also manifested in the publication of various handbooks (Grimm et al. 2020). A defining feature of most of the attention to security is that the focus is on the in/security of Northern-based contracting researchers. Discussions, handbooks and regulations tend to downplay not only the insecurities that facilitating researchers face, but also the roles we/they assume in assuring safety for contracting researchers.

As this book suggests, safety and security of contracting researchers cannot be realized at the cost of facilitating researchers who are the ones who tend to face the acute insecurities and precarities in the field. Moreover, as we will clearly demonstrate in this book, it is most often facilitating researchers who in reality assume the responsibilities for managing risks and assure safe access to the field – including the safety for contracting researchers. The role that facilitating researchers and their networks play in ensuring security and managing risks in the field is recognized in some literature (Hoffmann 2014; Kovats-Bernat 2002; Nordstrom 1997: xvii). Based on such observations, Kovats-Bernat for instance propose that 'researcher (read: "contracting") responsibility' should be replaced by the notion 'mutual responsibility'.

While mutual responsibility may capture the accurate situation and experiences in the field, it can still be problematic in suggesting that facilitating and contracting researchers somehow face equal risk and have equal access to measures to manage such risks (Eriksson Baaz and Utas 2019). We demonstrate in this book that facilitating researchers are more vulnerable to security risks and various other forms of precarities. We/they are more at risk since we/they are not seen as 'neutral' or disinterested parties but also as conflict insiders and implicated in conflicts on different sides. To add to these perceptions, we/they are also more at risk in the aftermath of data-collection, as we have no insurance, facilities and resources to mitigate new risks that emerge and appropriate evacuation plans. Moreover, as Chapter 5 of this book points out, 'risky/suspicious actions' by contracting researchers, can also expose facilitating researchers to extraordinary situations and risks (see Middleton and Pradhan 2014). Yet, much research funding allocations and planning make little or no allowances for the risks and vulnerabilities faced by facilitating researchers during and after the research.

Framing the North-South research relations and economic inequalities

The inequalities, extractive mindset and inherent colonial relations and legacies in North-South knowledge production and 'field research' have been discussed in several works. Borrowing neo-Marxist language, anthropologists Middleton and Cons for instance have succinctly argued that fieldwork labour 'cannot be divorced from the logics of capital' and that ethnographers 'with rare exceptions, (…) are in the business of transforming the work of the hired assistant into the cache of intellectual capital and acumen' (2014: 284). Middleton and Pradhan (2014: 358) raise similar issues emphasizing the 'subalternity' of research assistants. The relationship between 'assistants' and contracting researchers is conceptualized as an 'extraction surplus' that cannot 'fully be transcended'. More recently, Sukarieh and Tannocks (2019) have written about what they call the Syrian 'refugee research industry', using notions such as northern 'research capitalists' and the 'research proletariat' (Sukarieh and Tannocks 2019: 668). In their article they account for how this 'research proletariat' not only collect data and write up much research, but also are fully silenced or receiving little credit. In a blog recounting experiences of research in Uganda Mwambari and Owor (2019) use the term 'black market' to, in addition to other aspects, account for inequalities and practices in sensitive contexts where fieldwork is unregulated and where contracting researchers set their own standards and determine 'how money will be used, who is paid for what, and how much'. Similar accounts of inequalities and how facilitating researchers have to settle for little or even no remuneration, in the hope that the work they can open new opportunities for education or employment for them can also be found elsewhere (Cirhuza 2019, 2020; Cronin-Furman and Lake 2018; Mwambari and Owor 2019; Nshobole 2020). Yet, most discussions about workings of the unequal distribution of resources tend to remain on a general manner. As Bøås (2020) concludes, money matters in and for research relationships, but has remained the elephant in the room. The details of how levels of remuneration is calculated and agreed – or imposed on facilitating researchers – are something that almost never discussed anywhere in research-related literature, not even project proposals.

When questions of money and remuneration appear in the literature, contracting researchers sometimes emerge as the ones being vulnerable and exploited (see Eriksson Baaz and Utas 2019). In such accounts, facilitating researchers tend to be described as somehow extractive and greedy and as 'only interested in the money' (see Mudinga 2020). In some texts we/they are also portrayed as not fully able to understand or handle money matters in an appropriate manner and in need of instruction or even interventions when spending the money 'unwisely'. Molony and Hammett (2007: 297) for instance ask themselves if contracting researchers should 'hold back a percentage of the research assistant's income, or forward it to the wife when she/he sees that 'payment is being squandered on alcohol and prostitutes?' (Molony and Hammett 2007: 297). According to them, these kinds of financial issues and everyday life decisions that contracting researchers may have to make for the facilitating researchers can be tough on the former (2007: 287, see also Jenkins 2015). Such accounts of 'assistants' as 'only interested in, but not able to properly handle, money' do not only highlight the marked inequalities marking the relations, providing the contracting researcher the power to intervene by withholding money in the first place. They clearly also have a suspiciously familiar and colonial ring to them (see Eriksson Baaz 2005 for similar accounts in development work).

This book presents a quite different story, more in line with the concepts of 'black market' and 'extraction surplus' presented above. Yet, while the experiences of facilitating researchers in this book in large echo the literature that highlights inequalities, and at times outright exploitation, this is not the only story to be told. Engagement with contracting researchers can also lead to mutual dependencies, deep-ranging friendships and career opportunities, something we address in *Chapter 7: Beyond the bleak picture*.

Some additional notes on contexts, methodology and writing process

In this part, we will first provide some additional information about the three settings (DRC, Sierra Leone and India) and the contributors, followed by some further details about the writing process of this book, including some ethical reflections. As mentioned above, the project was arranged through workshops with facilitating researchers in the three settings. In the DRC the workshops were organized in 2019 in two settings, involving thirty participants, and in Sierra Leone one workshop was organized with fifteen facilitating researchers. Yet, due to the Covid pandemic the planned workshop set-up had to be abandoned in India and was instead replaced with individual interviews and a few focus groups (in total 25) conducted by Oseema Maria Toppo. Clearly, the book has no generalizing ambition. Yet, and drawing upon the literature cited above, we believe that the three different settings shed crucial light of various positions and arrangements surrounding facilitating research, which go beyond these sites in focus here.

An overview of the three settings

The post-conflict setting such as Sierra Leone provides an opportunity to situate facilitating researchers' experiences in a longer historical context, highlighting various routes when the demand reduces. In Sierra Leone, the workshops provided a novel opportunity to share and remember experiences. Most participating facilitating researchers started their/our brief or permanent careers during and in the years after, the civil/rebel war in Sierra Leone (1991–2001). During that time there was a glut of researchers, academic and others, coming from the North (chiefly Europe and UK) to conduct research in Sierra Leone. The workshop in Sierra Leone turned into a special event where the hours of the day are not enough, and dinner was pushed long into the night, remembering hardships and joys and how careers evolved over the years. The participants at the Sierra Leone workshop have few common denominators other than the fact that we/they have acted as facilitating researchers and that most are men. In the beginning, most external academic research attention was on conflict dynamics and such research entailed travelling into insecure areas, something which was often considered as too dangerous for women. Yet, after the war there has been an upsurge in women engaging in facilitating research. Otherwise, we/they were and are a diverse crowd: we were students, teachers, police officers and rebel soldiers; some were picked up randomly in our/their home villages; some volunteered; and others started doing research facilitation after recommendations by others. Some had university education already at that time, while some managed to get university education, in part because of our/their work with Northern-based researchers. Today the number of international researchers has dwindled as most were predominantly concerned with the armed conflict, not daily lives in peacetime.

By contrast, both the eastern DR Congo and Jharkhand in India are sites of ongoing – yet different – armed struggles. The eastern DR Congo has been a site of armed conflict for over two decades, with over 100 armed groups, from smaller village militias to professional rebel organizations, but also foreign armed groups. Hence, the facilitating researchers here are exposed to serious risks and much (though not all) of the research projects they engage in revolve around conflict dynamics and the ongoing violence. Common to most of the Congolese authors and participants is that we/they engage in research tasks on a temporary basis, depending on the access to research opportunities. As will be further developed in Chapter 2, most combine academic research tasks with, often a wide range of, other jobs and many are engaged to perform non-academic research tasks (i.e. monitoring, pre-studies, evaluations) by various humanitarian and development organizations. As will be accounted for in the book, some prefer performing such research tasks as remuneration and other work conditions are often better and up for negotiation, compared to research conducted with/for academic contracting researchers. While coming from different ethnic groups in the eastern DR Congo and having various levels of education, just like the groups in Sierra Leone, the researchers from quite a homogeneous group in terms of gender. Except for one woman, all others are men. The reason for this homogeneity is, in part, the same as in the Sierra Leone case. The relative absence of women among the writers is clearly a problem, particularly given that there certainly are Congolese women who act as facilitating researchers, often for other types of research projects not involving accessing areas of on-going armed conflict.

In Jharkhand, the abundance of natural resources and the insatiable appetite for extracting these natural resources have time and again led to fierce resistance from the local Adivasis (indigenous people), who are keen to preserve their land, natural resources, and distinct cultural and social milieu. While the history of Adivasi resistance to the exploiting classes goes back to the British Raj, it has manifested itself as the Naxalite movement, *Patthalgari* and other popular movements in the last few decades. Predictably, these resistance movements have drawn worldwide attention and engaged researchers in projects. The group of research facilitators from Jharkhand interviewed by Oseema Maria Toppo (in total 25) comprises a diverse set of people, aged between eighteen and seventy-five, spread across gender, class and ethnic categories. Yet, in contrast to the DRC and Sierra Leone, many are women and also engaged in issues related to women's rights. Among the people interviewed we find teachers, government employees, social activists, doctoral students, researchers and NGO activists.

The writing process of the book

The difference between the different settings – in additional to practical reasons – has informed the writing process. The main responsibility for drafting the six empirical chapters of the book was divided between the three countries involved, according to what the participants felt were most appropriate. For instance, as the DRC is still in a state of on-going armed conflict and high levels of insecurity, we/they took the main responsibility to draft the chapter focusing on in/security. Moreover, while experiences of exploitative research behaviour by more privileged researchers in and of the 'Global South' were experienced in all settings, this theme was particularly accentuated by the facilitating researchers in India who, for that reason, were given the main responsibility for drafting that chapter. Similarly, the facilitating researchers in Sierra Leone resumed responsibility for Chapter 7: *Beyond the bleak picture,* as they have a longer historical perspective and in the workshops reflected much on the relationships we/they developed with contracting researchers and how some of those enabled us/them to access educational opportunities, research skills and professional networks. Yet, all chapters include comments from authors in the two other countries, highlighting differences and similarities across contexts.

Co-authorship was promised to all participants in the workshops willing to appear as co-authors. In the DR Congo and Sierra Leone most workshop participants wished to appear as co-authors. In India, the situation was more complex, and based on requests for anonymity. Oseema Maria Toppo agreed to be the sole author of these chapters. Due to practical reasons, the drafting of the six empirical chapters – which are written in a we-form – was undertaken by Abedi Dunia, Vincent and Toppo, drawing upon the transcripts of the workshops. In order to facilitate the writing of the texts and also arrange for communication and translation between English- and French-speaking writers, Karin Elfving was engaged in the project and has also assisted in drafting some of the chapters together with Abedi Dunia. Yet, all people listed as co-authors of the various chapters are to be regarded as actual authors, both as the texts are based on their testimonies and writings in the workshops and as they have provided inputs on the chapter drafts.

As the readers will notice, the tone and writing style of the chapters vary a bit. This is a result of the writing styles of the various authors and should be seen as a reflection of the participatory process that the book is based upon. Moreover, and as a reader of all the chapters may note, there are also some overlaps between the chapters. This is an unavoidable consequence, not only of the writing processes, but also of how the various themes of the chapters are intimately connected and cannot be easily separated. For instance, the theme of being silenced and neglected, or the theme of insecurities runs through and is deeply connected also to other experiences/themes.

Some reflections on research ethics

Most of the authors of the book share the belief that the problem of unequal, and at times exploitative, research relations mainly has its roots in structural causes and inequalities, even if individual qualities of researchers also play a role. This will be developed in the concluding chapter. While some would argue that a strategy of naming and shaming individual researcher can bring about change, this book avoids such a strategy from the perspective of research ethics. In order to ensure that individual researchers or other people cannot be identified we have – when concrete stories/examples are portrayed – changed the names of people and locations and altered other potential identity markers such as age, gender and affiliation. At times and when deemed necessary, we have also slightly altered the stories told. This applies in particular to events that we know are quite uncommon and where (parts of) the event/story is well known and have been circulated among other researchers. Yet, such strategies with the aim of ensuring anonymity are always fraught with difficulties, not the least as the new identity markers in the stories might accidentally hint at other people that we are not aware of. For that reason, and with the hope that we have been at least somehow successful in our strategies, we urge the readers who feel that they can identify themselves or a colleague, keep in mind that this is unlikely the case, and simply and hopefully a result of unlucky rewriting/circumstances.

Outline of the book

Chapter 2: *Getting and keeping engaged*, written mainly by the authors/researchers in Sierra Leone, addresses the highly diverse backgrounds of facilitating/brokering researchers (various previous occupations, such as journalists, university lecturers, students, NGO workers, politicians, former combatants, etc.). It also highlights how facilitating researchers engage in research on a more temporary basis, while some have been able to turn research facilitation into a more regular occupation. The chapter describes how many researchers play multiple roles, simultaneously facilitating the work of a range of actors. It also discusses the difference between engaging in facilitation in relation to research and other actors whom some of us also facilitate, such as journalists, UN missions and various humanitarian actors. While experiences differ, the main conclusion is that contracting researchers/academics are most often not offering better conditions than other actors, on the contrary. This chapter also addresses the various ways in which facilitating research is organized. As the other chapters, this chapter will also include comments from authors in the two other countries (DR Congo and India).

Chapter 3: *The indispensable bridge: Without us no research*, written mainly by the authors/researchers in the DR Congo, addresses the various roles that facilitating researchers occupy. As this chapter will show, the concept of facilitating researcher is somehow misleading, as so much of the work consists of tasks outside the supposed core of our/ their research task, namely data collection itself, and as the roles in part instead at times tend to become that of research management: managing research before, during and after data collection. Importantly, the work performed is much more varied and complex than what is stated in the contracts (in the cases there are contracts). As demonstrated in this chapter, facilitating researchers in the eastern DR Congo perform various tasks additional to data collection, such as preparing for the field visits, preparing access to the field and identifying informants, arranging meetings with various local authorities, managing expectations of respondents and others, making and managing itineraries under tight schedules, preparing/adjusting research tools, interpretation and translation of the collected data and managing the after-work of fieldwork. As the other chapters, this chapter will also include reflections and additions from authors in the two other countries (i.e. Sierra Leone and India).

Chapter 4: *Systematically silenced and non-recognized*, written by Toppo, addresses the systematic silencing of facilitating researchers; how we/they rarely make it further than the acknowledgement section (sometimes not even that) and have slim chances of appearing as co-authors. It also shows how facilitating researchers often only are provided with very limited information about the research they are engaged with. In addition to that, the chapter retells many other experiences of broken promises, such as contracting researchers disappearing without a trace after fieldwork, broken promises of remuneration and career opportunities, but also a lack of what is experienced as staged and fake compassion and respect of research subjects. The chapter also discusses the fear of speaking out due to the power inequalities. As the other chapters, this chapter also includes comments and reflections from authors in the two other countries (i.e. Sierra Leone and the DR Congo).

Chapter 5: *Managing various aspects of insecurity*, written mainly by authors from the DR Congo, addresses how facilitating researchers try to manage various forms of insecurities. Yet, in contrast to what might be assumed (given that the book focuses on insecure settings), the chapter does not address the insecurity experienced in relation to conducting research in the midst of the ongoing armed conflicts only. While the exposure to a range of risks, such as arrests, beatings and threats, is a theme addressed in the chapter it is emphasized that these are not the only insecurities faced. In contrast to most contracting researchers, most facilitating researchers do not have a stable income that is sufficient to cover daily expenses. This aspect of insecurity will also feature in this chapter, not simply because it reflects the realities of facilitating researchers, but as it also is deeply related to our/their exposure to the risks connected to the insecure setting linked to the ongoing armed conflicts. As will be described in this chapter, it reduces the ability to negotiate and forces facilitating researchers to take risks in order to secure an income. Yet also the reverse is true. While conducting facilitating research clearly provides an income, conducting research in risky environments is often very costly. As the Congolese authors will demonstrate in this chapter, we/they often have to cover such expenses from our/their own pockets. As the other chapters, this chapter also includes comments and reflections from authors in the two other countries (i.e. Sierra Leone and India).

While most of the chapters focus on contracting researchers based in the Global North and thus, reflect the continued marked inequalities in North-South relations, Chapter 6: *Beyond a narrow South/North divide*, written mainly by the researchers in India, highlights the need to think beyond a narrow South/North divide. It highlights how the marked inequalities between facilitating/brokering researchers and contracting researchers also take place within national contexts. In short, it shows how exploitative research behaviour is prevalent among more privileged researchers in and of the 'Global South'. It demonstrates how national contracting researchers often engage in a similar – or even worse – behaviour as those from outside in order to further their own research. It also shows how national contracting researchers may capitalize on their roles as intermediaries between contracting researchers in the Global North and facilitating/brokering researchers engaged locally, in an exploitative manner. As the other chapters, this chapter will also include comments and reflections from authors in the two other countries (i.e. Sierra Leone and the DR Congo).

The book, in general, highlights glaring inequalities and exploitative relations, but this is of course not always the case. Engagement with contracting researchers can also lead to mutual dependencies, deep-ranging friendships and career opportunities. Chapter 7: *Beyond the bleak picture*, written mainly by the researchers in Sierra Leone, addresses such experiences and what seems to make those possible. The chapter includes narratives of trust building, how relationships we/they developed with contracting researchers have enabled some to simultaneously improve educational standard and research skills, but also professional networks and how some of these professional relationships have transformed into deep friendships over the years. As the other chapters, this chapter will also include comments and reflections from authors in the two other countries (i.e. India and the DR Congo).

The last chapter, Chapter 8: *The need of change: What, how and who?*, starts with a brief analysis of the factors contributing to the problems highlighted in the chapters in the book, locating these in the colonial legacy of research and continued stark inequalities of North/South relations in knowledge production. In particular, it emphasizes unequal funding structures, but also the general hierarchical and unequal structures within, as well as the increasing neo-liberalization of academia. The following part of the chapter proposes some routes, for change. It argues for the need to recognize that the contribution that many facilitating/brokering researchers make not only merits co-authorship, but often also makes non-authorship both fraudulent and unethical. It also emphasizes the need for better and a more transparent remuneration policy in agreements, where the compensation is open for negotiation and reflects the level of risk. A central argument in the chapter is that change requires much more than appealing to the consciousness of individual researchers. A more comprehensive approach in which various key actors, such as funding agencies and ethics board and committees assessing projects, take responsibility and press for change is sorely needed. Academic publishers also have a great responsibility and role to play in effectuating change. Like funders and ethic review boards, they need to ask questions about the role and situation of brokering researchers before approval of publication. Yet, the chapter also discusses and outlines various strategies that facilitating researchers themselves can engage in, in order to initiate change.

2

Getting and keeping engaged

James B. M. Vincent, Abdul Hakeem Mansaray, Abu Bakarr Jaward, Marion Anita Rogers and Aisha Kamara

T was a young former combatant who was asked to assist a team of Danish researchers. With a poor rural upbringing and currently living on the very margins of urban Freetown, T had never been very close to white people. When they picked him up in a big white Land Cruiser in downtown Freetown, he was quite anxious. There were four white men in the car, apart from T. Instead of taking the normal road out of the city the car branched off and took a road unknown to T. This is when he really started to worry. Where were they taking him? T knew that Denmark has a common border with Germany. Although he was not educated in school beyond a point, he knew that Germans did many cruel things during the Second World War. As his stress built up, he started to think that maybe Danes were equally dangerous; maybe (were they?) even carrying out cannibalistic rituals. His stomach started to turn, what if they killed him? After a quick risk analysis, he faked illness and made them stop the car. Whilst they continued their journey, T found his way back to the safety of Freetown. No harm inflicted.

The story of T was circulated during a two-day workshop (October 2019) held in Sierra Leone, where we focused on our experiences of working as facilitating researchers during and after the Sierra Leonean civil war (1991–2001). While we may have laughed at the story,[1] since

---

[1] Equally facetious is the fact that at times we come across contracting researchers from the Global North, who value rumours of cannibalism in Sierra Leone as a real threat to their security.

it was rather extreme, it was still indicative of some of the uncertainties that junior or rural facilitating researchers experience when they start working with contracting researchers from the Global North. Suffice it to say, T never ventured into this line of work again, unlike us, the participants in the workshop upon whose experience this chapter is based.

As mentioned in the introductory chapter, we were fourteen in number, predominantly men, but with a few women, from all walks of life, originating from across the country. Some of us had university education, some managed to get university education because of our work with contracting researchers from the Global North. Some of us were picked up randomly in our home villages, some of us volunteered, and others started doing research facilitation because they were recommended by others. Some were students, teachers, police officers and past rebel soldiers. As a group we come from diverse socio-financial, religious, economic and educational circumstances, with varying cultural, religious and traditional backgrounds and beliefs. We came from the capital city, provincial cities, smaller towns of the interior and small rural villages. Now we also had diverse occupations: university lecturers, teachers, students, civil servants, active national and international NGOs and businesspersons. We had few common denominators other than the fact that we helped contracting researchers in carrying out their jobs. Today our cadre is semi-professional, although the number of international researchers has dwindled, as a good number of them were predominantly concerned with our conflicts, not our daily lives in peacetime.

In this chapter, we will account for the various ways in which we were engaged and how our work and situation have evolved over time. 'We' also need to be careful with the notion of 'we' here since our experiences and current situations differ. While some of us, as will be mentioned in this chapter, and also further elaborated in Chapter 7, have benefited quite greatly from our work as facilitating researchers, some have benefited less and mainly have negative experiences. Also, some of us did not really understand how badly we had been treated by some, until we could compare our experiences with others. Hence, the workshop was indeed a very useful experience.

The chapter will proceed as follows. We will start with a few stories of how we first got engaged in this work. After this we will provide a short overview of how the situation has changed over the years. In contrast to the cases of the DR Congo and Jharkhand (India), Sierra Leone can provide a useful insight into how the work of facilitating researchers can change over time, from conflict, post-conflict to more secure settings – even though work we conducted during Ebola crises, ravaging the country in 2014–15, in part resembled the years of armed conflict. This is followed by a short account of how many of us simultaneously facilitated the work of a range of actors, such as journalists, UN missions and various humanitarian actors and how that relates and compares to facilitating research with academics. (Here we also address the various ways in which brokering research is organized and how it is in some contexts commercialized; for instance, through the development of consultancy groups and individual consultants that provide brokering services for research).

A changing landscape: War and post war

Most of us started this line of work during the war. Our field experiences varied quite a lot depending on the community we focused on. A community in urban Freetown and for instance rural Kailahun can be worlds apart. Different types of communities have various security arrangements depending on the needs of the people, the chief and community elders, the government orders, and at times influences of a powerful rebel group, militia or military brigade (either ECOMOG/UN peacekeepers or the Sierra Leone army). Our experiences therefore were many and varied in nature. Changes during the war could occur on a daily basis. A facilitating researcher may work convivially in a peaceful community and inform a colleague that it is safe and when the colleague comes around a few weeks later, it is quite the opposite. Moreover, the local contact person safeguarding the previous group may have moved on or could even have been killed. During the height of the war, security could even change radically and drastically in a day. Sometimes we start going about work peacefully and hours later we are asked to leave immediately as there is an imminent rebel, CDF or government forces attack later in the day. These were days when security was truly fluid and unpredictable as the situation report could change in the twinkle of an eye. At times our colleagues were trapped in villages under attack, or roads they needed to travel were blocked for longer periods. During the war, facilitating research work entailed a lot of dangers.

In the pre-war situation contracting researchers rarely needed full-time facilitating researchers as the country was safe. The war created not just an upsurge in research, but also an increase in the need and demand for facilitating researchers. Pre-war contracting researchers only needed an official guide from the office of the NGO, or a contact at the local university, that brought them out into the provinces or Western Area (rural or urban). Many contracting researchers moved around, worked and settled all by themselves. In the local communities they were often perceived as Peace Corps volunteers. They moved around and conducted meetings with no fear and with not too many challenges. The official guides however needed to know the community norms and entry requirements, and these varied from one community or locality, ethnic group, or region to another. During the war cultural differences over areas and ethnic groups became more important, as for instance ethnic militias, or civil defence forces, were moulded partly around cultural traits and knowledge.

However, during the war, contracting researchers who came in demanded facilitating researchers who were street smart, flexible, well grounded and knowledgeable of the areas to be visited. Being well-connected and respected in the local communities was pivotal not only for safety reasons, but also in order to collect reliable data. Having local knowledge ensured that the contracting researcher was not tricked by political propaganda and bias. Most facilitating researchers were highly knowledgeable with the terrain in the places they were working.

A successful facilitating researcher would brief the contracting researcher about the security situation on the ground in the areas they were going to cover. His/her knowledge and acquaintances were also of help when unforeseen problems occurred. It is worth noting that during this period, the military commander's advice superseded even though we still had to crosscheck with the locals and the militia group operating in the area. As contributors from other countries in this volume also give account of, doing research in war-affected countries, where an active civil conflict/war was ongoing, is both extremely complex and risky.

Immediately after the end of the war in 2003, when some sort of rule of law had been restored, Sierra Leone saw many researchers who came in for a few weeks only, but some settled-in for extended periods. International research interest for our tiny country boomed and facilitating research work was at times sizeable and challenging. Many new willing and inexperienced facilitating researchers entered the trade. Even then, many parts of the country remained insecure and fragile, thus a big chunk of our work was still guiding, protecting and securing the contracting researchers. We kept daily briefing exercises on the security situation, arranging security clearances in their stead from the police, military or other security operatives in that particular area. In short, we thus maintained our roles as moral and security guarantors for them during the period of their stay in country. In such circumstances, we started finding real trust and confidence in ourselves, and thus changing the dynamics between the contracting researchers from the Global North and research facilitators from the Global South. Partly due to the large numbers of contracting researchers entering the country on the one hand, and partly due to a more organized society on the other hand, we had the opportunity of organizing, creating networks and at times (the more qualified and field tested facilitating researchers) taking on more direct research roles. By improving networks and organization, we also managed to jointly put pressure on the contracting researchers and thereby improve our working conditions to a considerable extent. That said, it is still quite common that some of us work without proper contracts and/or not fully knowing what our work contains. Many times, we see this as a real form of exploitation:

> *Delaying or not signing a contract, that's a way of exploiting. Because if you go into the field without signing, you will not know. There can be things in the ToR that you don't have in mind, because you haven't signed yet. So then they can benefit and afterwards they give you the contract to sign. I think that is exploitation.*

This statement during the workshop was quickly followed by another one of us:

> *Some of the researchers we work with, you actually don't know how much they will pay. They will give you some advance money, and you go to do the study. By the end, they give you money. Some will just pay you, some will not even sign a paper for the amount of money you received.*

Signing contracts was a contentious issue that we discussed throughout the workshop. We have all felt cheated at least once. One of us also had the experience of having to sign for an amount that was not given to him. This was a UNDP-sponsored project subcontracted to a local organization. When he was about to sign, they said, 'If you want the money you sign, if you don't you don't'. In the end, he agreed to sign for four million Leones, but only received half of the amount.

In the present circumstances, it is a requirement from the Ministry of Development and Economic Planning that researchers must have in-country collaborators to undertake especially long-term research work. The collaborator will be called in for questioning should there be any misinformation in any report that goes international. Security is much improved and well-structured now with the Office of National Security (ONS) fully in-charge and on a local level there are provincial and district security apparatus. The latter bodies work under the Office of the President for the coordination of internal and external security. For now, the facilitating researchers have the responsibility to inform the security apparatus if they want to visit any area that is marked sensitive, especially when there is tension around chiefdom elections or other local political problems. This is because, the political dynamics has changed completely in most parts of the country. Virtually every activity has been somehow politicized. (You are either supporting the ruling party or the opposition at any point in time.) The facilitating researchers are sometimes put under unnecessary pressure when working in some areas especially if you are not born and bred in that community or district. The language could also be a concern, as they easily connive and hide pertinent information from you and lead you to make conclusions that may be questioned by academics and other individuals coming from that particular community or district. You can experience challenges in getting information for simply not talking the dominant language in that area. Yet at times, we have experienced contracting researchers who ignore the importance of knowing language. This topic came to the fore during our workshop, where for instance one of us critically stated:

> *But you, the international people, you will recruit anyone. You will recruit me and take me to Makeni, but I am not Temne; I don't speak the language. I will collect data for you, but it will not be too accurate.*

Facilitating researchers with the right language skills would do a better job; nevertheless, most of us would accept a job offer like that simply because it would render us an income.

How we got engaged in this line of work and how we evolved

Most, if not all of us, facilitating researchers started brief or permanent careers during the civil war. We were young, some of us still in our teens, predominantly without kids, and many struggled with paying school or university fees. 'As a student it was very attractive to do this thing', one of us indicated during the workshop. Work as facilitating researchers was quite often part of an effort of upward social mobility and as means to secure funds for school fees. The latter was a struggle many contracting researchers could relate to.

Contracting researchers came as individuals from predominantly Europe, UK and United States, but also from Japan, India and Brazil. Some came from prominent academic institutions such as Oxford, LSE and Harvard to name a few. As facilitating researchers, we have worked with some of the most high-profile international professors in conflict studies, IR political science, economics and anthropology.

Some contracting researchers stayed only for a few weeks; they were often consultants, or researchers doing empirical research using quantitative methods as the dominant approach. They arrived alone or in teams and often had coordinated their activities with Sierra Leonean or international organizations beforehand. We got contracted either directly or by the local organization. Other contracting researchers, researchers or students doing an MA or PhD with university affiliation, were more field research oriented and stayed for longer periods between a month up to a year, or even two. Those who stayed longest were generally anthropologists. Notwithstanding academic discipline, they all needed some help. Some were informally aided, whilst others organized assistance in a more formal way. Some paid tokens, others paid quite well. Some came, left quickly, disappeared, whilst others became our friends and acquaintances. Although some of our employers worked in the humanitarian aid organizations, or for international organizations, a good number were academic researchers, predominantly from universities in the Global North. However, we also have experiences of researchers from the sub-region, such as Nigeria, or from our own country for that matter.

'I have worked with many researchers from within social work, health, politics, anthropologists, economists and one journalist', stated one of us during the workshop. Contracting researchers, during and in the direct aftermath of the war, were from a wide range of disciplines, but dominated by political scientists/peace and conflict researchers/IR and anthropologists. Many of the researchers we worked with were early in their careers; they were masters or PhD students. But others were senior scholars. Today most of them are well-known names in academia. In fact, when Mats, the scholar who initiated this project in Sierra Leone, talked us through the most known scholars in the study of conflict and post conflict Sierra Leone, we had with few exceptions worked with them, or at least we knew someone who had. Some of us have only worked with a handful of researchers, but the most experienced of us had worked with close to forty.

Most contracting researchers look for a soft landing, but can be nice, fair and respectful if treated with respect and provided with prudent and strategic pieces of advice or information and with the requisite qualification and experience of the facilitating researchers. Their needs are many and varied and we have aided them by locating knowledge on research topics as diverse as: history, social and cultural issues, economy and finances, peace and conflict prevention and resolution, conservation, re-construction, development, disarmament and demobilization, community participation, decentralization and democratic processes, issues of gender and sexuality, food security, agricultural systems, mining economies, fishing and more recently in the aftermath of the Ebola epidemic a lot of projects centering health and health systems. Without doubt, we have only included half of the topics we have conducted research on, but it suffices to say that even if some of us have become more specialized in one field, and others in another, our work as facilitating researchers has turned us into experts of many fields – or as a Jack of all trades, as the popular adage says. At the same time, it also shows the fragility of a research system where a contracting researcher is often tremendously dependent on the skills, but also will, of facilitating researchers. The latter was mentioned several times during the workshop, relating to how the effort of the contracting researchers influenced the quality of the work on the side of the facilitating researcher. One of us noted:

> *You must care for people first. You can't just go and take something from them. If something goes wrong, this is most likely the reason. If I don't like you, I can start to distort information. It doesn't need to be intentional, but I will make less effort.*

So how then did we get involved in this work? As concluded above, while our differences may be greater now than when most of us started, it still differed already then. We will provide two examples of how it started, pinpointing different backgrounds.

Story 1

During our Senior Secondary School (SSS) days, a woman from a European country who was doing research for her master's degree on war-affected persons turned up at our school compound. At the time, the project *Children Associated with the War* (CAW) took care of us and assisted us in going to school. A schoolmate recommended the woman to talk to me as I was formerly a small boy *Kamajor* [a southeastern civil defence force]. There were also *Revolutionary United Front* (RUF) fighters in school. She picked me, and a former RUF fighter, to assist her in her work.

I helped her navigate in our community and its environs. We went to several villages, and I served mainly as an interpreter, helping her with logistics, and acted as an intermediary (now referred to as facilitating researcher-FR). She completed her research and promised that she would advocate on our behalf to get some funds to come and help the community and those of us who assisted her in her study. She gave us $200 for the whole period of the research exercise. This was because, we were hoping we would get education through her efforts when she came back in a few months' time. When she revisited us after five months she brought in an NGO called *Mind to Change*. This project paid our school fees, provided uniforms up to the time we sat for our *West Africa senior school certificate examination* (WASSCE). However, after she left, I could not pursue my education further because, I did not have money to pay for school expenses.

Fortunately, this woman returned to Sierra Leone, and I explained my struggles and predicaments to her. At this point she could only help me start a small business selling mobile top-up cards. Yet, with this money I managed to get a *Higher National Diploma* (HND) in accounting and finance. Before she left again, she introduced me to another researcher who came to work on the theme 'The end of evil'. This was about secret societies and cultism. He also did fieldwork in Liberia, Guinea and India. I took him to my home village where we researched the secret societies. He asked people to perform permissible rituals [there are many rituals only performed to initiates of the secret societies] in front of him and he took photos. We toured the country together and I helped him coordinate all the movement as far as into neighbouring Liberia.

Story 2

I started research by default in 1995 when I did some work with a young researcher from a European country. He became my main mentor. He introduced me to research by encouraging me to be with him and taking notes whilst he conducted interviews with dignitaries and government officials, I had made prior appointments with. During the war period it was mainly in the larger towns, which were relatively safe during those periods. I was basically a first-degree graduate in agriculture, a driver and a fixer arranging meetings for him. I was then in my late twenties. I had an old car that I rented out for less money than the taxis in town. The fee of $40 a day also included my fixer abilities. At the time, I was fine with that. After a while, I demonstrated good skills, and he decided to take me in as a regular research assistant (facilitating researcher) and he paid me a reasonable emolument (in the region of about $50 per day for work during the next few years).[2] We jointly researched the influences of the rebel war on the economy of Sierra Leone and especially on the living standards of the rural

---

[2] We want to acknowledge that this fee is rather high. Many others received, and still receive less. In general, it seems like facilitating researchers in Sierra Leone receive a slightly higher remuneration than what the DR Congo colleagues have informed us about in Chapter 5.

population. He taught me my first interview skills. Later on, I was privileged to work with a more experienced researcher/consultant on issues relating to agriculture and social issues. My first mentor was a professor, and he had many contacts, which proved to be a blessing for me later on in life. In all honesty, I learnt a lot from the research skills of the contracting researchers I worked for in the coming few years, but I couldn't help to feel clear disadvantages and differences between me and them. I would for instance arrange meetings, prepare the ground and do detailed preparations to make sure meetings would be perfect. I would develop meeting agendas, but when it was time for the meeting, I was left out sitting with the secretary or roaming around in the office area wondering what they talked about. Sometimes I felt it was humiliating, but other times, especially if they had meetings with high-profile politicians, diplomats or INGO staff, I started getting suspicious that they were discussing anti-Sierra Leone, or government issues that were sensitive and did not want me to hear what was going on. However, on a few occasions I was lucky to be called in by the very dignitaries when we were setting up the appointments. Quite often they enjoyed our discussions because I had a lot of 'local knowledge' which they (the contracting researchers) lacked.

Later, through one of these contacts, I was employed as a consultant for managing war-affected youths and former combatants. This exposed me to knowledge of the war, which few others in my position had. Starting out with these experiences, I have learnt to multi-task, crisscross between consultancy work and short-term NGO employment, working with INGOs and university professors. I have become a Jack-of-all-trades doing work for historians one month and biologists the next. On top of basic abilities to hook contracting researchers up with the right persons in the field, and sufficiently good understanding of the specific context of the specific study, I have added rich experiences of analysing data, relating findings to previous findings and as such made facilitating research work into a trade that I master and make a living from.

Current experiences: Juggling and organizing various jobs

Even those of us who have a credible academic background and a full-time job often end up becoming dependent on consultancy work. With a poor salary structure in the country, some of us prefer waiting for contracting researchers to come along rather than having to work for twenty-six days a month as a civil servant and being paid a mere $120. Some facilitating researchers have made it to the point where they have transformed facilitating research and consultancy work into full-time in a very short time. This is, unfortunately, only true for those with higher education. Most, except a few, of us do assignments as facilitating researchers as a part-time employment and thus have to cater to other jobs in-between, a factor that contributes to our vulnerability.

During the direct aftermath of the war (and more recently again after the Ebola outbreak) quite a few of us had busy schedules and dependable incomes. There have been some attempts to establish Freetown-based firms/local NGOs dedicated to working with contracting researchers on study and evaluation consultancies. In such cases, there have been strategic efforts to tie up with international NGOs, UN agencies, but also local government structures such as the Ministries (education, health, interior, agriculture, defence, local government, social welfare and gender and children's affairs, etc., and Statistics Sierra Leone). Such structures, amongst other things, make it easier to participate in bidding processes (which does not apply to academic research though). Although there are some clear advantages, we, the facilitating researchers in this study, have chosen instead to organize in more informal network-like structures, where we partly help each other, but also partly compete over work.

At times, education may not be the most important asset in relationship to local communities. Sometimes quite the opposite, it can be a hindrance. Yet still, we see it as central in order to build a good command and rapport with the contracting researchers. When we are hired, our educational background is, together with knowing the area of study, the most important aspect. Many of us see facilitating research work as an educational journey. Not only do we learn new things during our missions, but the work often gives us opportunities of furthering our education. During the period of carrying out facilitating research duties, several of us have managed to obtain master's degrees, and two have even been aided in getting education abroad. One statement from our workshop makes this point:

> So this researcher first financed my college studies in political science. She actually helped me. She sponsored me throughout, up until now when I write my thesis in sociology.

Still many facilitating researchers are junior secondary or senior secondary school pass outs only and therefore can easily be swayed by a few dollars or euros for carrying out work that can be dangerous, but also ethically questionable. One of us was for instance given money to buy drugs in order to get access to a drugs cartel, an act that enhanced the contracting researcher's access to vital data for his work, but which was at the same time highly immoral, especially as the facilitating researcher was an ex-combatant with a troubled past, and not in a position to deny the contracting researcher such tasks. During the war, several of us had gone deeper into rebel territory because the contracting researchers have pushed us to and been at risk. We took a lot of responsibility for the safety of contracting researchers, but we rarely saw the opposite. Our experiences hold that they don't consider our security as a problem because this is our country and there is a naïve idea that it is therefore not a dangerous place for us!

We realized the fact that many of us had not been treated fairly when we came into contact with a colleague who had prior experience working with a fair contracting researcher. At that point furthering our education became a weapon for fighting for our rights and hindering exploitation. Especially during the war years with all the poverty and uncertainty, it became an uphill struggle. Because of these challenges we had jointly worked on educating ourselves to know certain basic rights and responsibilities when needed, that we ought to take into consideration when working with contracting researchers. We have made it clear that contracting researchers are not our enemies, and some have facilitated our careers (see Chapter 7).

Some facilitating researchers are highly qualified, and we consider them, albeit informally, our senior brothers and sisters. This is not because of age but rather because of experience, network and the general leverage their involvement brings to the group. Their long-term experience often combined with educational level makes them suited for initial contacts and negotiation with contracting researchers. Their presence gives junior ones a sense of security, protection if not confidence, that is required to carry out our tasks. Working with a white contracting researcher, especially the first time, was for most of us an experience of excitement and worry if not fear. Working with white men/women, be they researchers or visitors, gave us respect and class in the eyes of many in the local community. Even though it was advantageous, it also created problems for us, as one stated during the workshop.

When I was assisting this woman in Kenema and I went to school. All my friends in school thought I got a lot of money from her. 'I see you with the white man', some people admire you so much because you are with a white person.

A constant hassle has been that family and friends believe that working with foreign contracting researchers rendered almost instant wealth and all of us have struggled to make people understand that research facilitation especially during the war years and its early aftermath was oftentimes not well paid.

However, more so, it meant that we got 'exposed' to the larger world, with education and progress. At least that was what we first thought. Yet it was also a somewhat daunting task as society, unfortunately, had taught us that we were not qualified to work with 'advanced' white people. From childhood we are taught not to trust white people. But at the same time, there is a very strong inferiority complex in our society, especially in the rural areas, as some of us pointed out during the workshop:

In the villages they get perceptions of white people. White people have money. They have power. They think that white people are more intelligent than black. They feel pride if a white person shake their hands, play with their children. It is like a minister comes from Freetown. It is the same level.

With more education we now understand that colonialism cemented our sense of inferiority, something our society still battles with. A mutual distrust persists. Navigating such complex structures for many of us would not have been possible, had we been left alone without knowledge. We could have ended up in a bizarre situation like 'T' in the vignette this chapter started with. Thus, in addition to helping us to link up with contracting researchers, organizing contracts, senior facilitating researchers guide us in the field. They also help us understand and situate the contracting researchers, how they work, what they need and how they relate to us. Our networks do not work like a company, but we help each other in multiple ways. Networks create opportunities and mutual dependencies. It makes facilitating research jobs work.

As facilitating researchers, we also contribute to research projects headed by UN, EU, World Bank and their multi-lateral missions. Furthermore, we have worked with reputable multi- and bi-lateral research groups put together by donor institutions like the World Bank group, the European Union, DFID, other donors like DANIDA, Sida, CIDA, and highly regarded INGOs like CARE, World Vision International and CRS. Working with these types of institutions or organizations gives us more contacts by building our networks and as such access to more contracting researchers with time. They also in most cases pay better than individual or private contracting researchers who come alone and whose budgets are very low quite often. With these organizations/institutions, they consider several other parameters including better allowances, security, insurance, sometimes good arrangements with regard to medical facilities and physical conditions when working in the field, opportunities for evacuation when needed and some cash available for miscellaneous expenditure. However, there are exceptions to every rule. At the time of the workshop two of us worked for a medical NGO where we had negative experiences with the head of the organization, a European medical doctor. In the words of one of us:

> I am currently working with a white doctor (working for an international NGO). She is against the black. But we have to endure, because we need the money. She is discriminatory and even if she has got the resources she will underpay us. Right now she has cut the salary, so we only get 50 USD per month.

Some of us communicate with higher cadres of stakeholders from our government, like ministers, permanent secretaries and the likes and the more experienced facilitating researchers may lead some of the policy processes of theirs. Some of us also worked with journalists. However, working with academics is far more beneficial and gainful in comparison. Academics are generally willing to teach us their skills and ensure that they do not embarrass you. International journalists on the other hand will always put you on the edge until you see or hear the report on international news media. In some instances, we have been questioned by government officials whom we had interviewed to explain why a certain report had been written about the country (a question, you cannot easily answer).

It should also be mentioned that for many of us, the experience of working in larger teams of researchers from various countries and continents from the global south, who speak different languages was and is rather different. From some perspectives, they are always a more reasonable group to work with and it gives us another position. There were always checks and balances due to the fact that the group had highly qualified and experienced professors/contracting researchers made up of people with PhD and master's degrees who were desirous to work and excel so that they could attract more funding, build up their reputation and create the necessary impact. We believe that large multicultural team triggered a reasonable treatment to facilitating researchers and contracting researchers, as it diffused some of the marked power differences of traditional North-South collaboration.

Another benefit was that it opened up for new ways of understanding research findings beyond the normal European tropes.

In developing countries, we are faced with enormous challenges and dilemmas both in our relationships with our more senior colleagues (contracting researchers) and in the execution of their tasks in our various areas of operation. For a very long time, the research world has been indifferent to our challenges, problems, pressures, flashbacks and sufferings we experience in the field during research. One of our colleagues said, 'We sometimes consider ourselves as a forgotten group who despite our significance have been and are still contributing immensely to ongoing research in our country, research and researchers globally.'

Fieldwork in a country like Sierra Leone has some rather specific qualities. Firstly, the contracting researcher quite commonly does not come from the country and has seldom any deeper knowledge of the context in which the research takes place. This is the basis for a rare relationship between contracting researcher and facilitating researcher in our setting. Although from a financial point of view the contracting researcher has a clear upper hand, there is another imbalance when it comes to knowledge where the facilitating researcher often is the one who has the wealth of knowledge. Quite often we have experienced that contracting researchers, despite at times being full professors, may need a lot of assistance even with the simplest of tasks, placing them in rather vulnerable, and even subordinate positions, when in the field. This, we gather, creates rather unbalanced relationships when doing research in our part of the world, compared to fields both contracting researchers and facilitating researchers are native to. However, there is a pronounced difference between a contracting researcher from the North, with a stable position within a university or an international organization and with a salary that is exorbitantly higher, and that of a facilitating researcher in a fragile life realm like that of Sierra Leone. Adding a postcolonial perspective on power and status differences adds to the uneven work situation that we found ourselves in. A third issue adding to this is that many of us come from poor rural backgrounds, are young (at least when we started facilitating research work) and have fought hard to educate ourselves. Becoming a facilitating researcher is often seen as a golden opportunity enabling upward social mobility and furthering our education. Such vulnerable position leaves the field wide open to exploitative relations. At times we offer virtually pro-bono work to the researchers with the hope that they will help us in future. Sometimes, a few of our northern counterparts are so insensitive to our plight that they pretend not to know that they ought to pay us for our work.

Reflections from Jharkhand/India: More alternate employments and women
By Anju Oseema Maria Toppo

The indigenous people's culture, history, tradition and lifestyle have always attracted the scholars' intellectual curiosity worldwide. Consequently, in order to conduct research, scholars from across the globe visit Jharkhand, the home to a sizeable population of Adivasis in India. As these researchers descend in Jharkhand, we, the facilitating researchers, emerge as the most cherished allies for them. Like the facilitating researchers from Sierra Leone, we too have been generous, propitious and meritorious contributors to several research projects. However, much like our colleagues in Sierra Leone, we too are denied due recognition or fitting rewards for our diligence and hard work. Through the research work in Jharkhand, several of the visiting researchers have acquired considerable fame; however, we realize that our knowledge and expertise on the local issues are far greater than the ostensible high-profile researchers.

Our scope of work is not limited to assisting the researcher; instead, we are accountable for making appropriate contacts in the field and, more importantly, for navigating through several of the bureaucratic, political and social faultiness. Our responsibilities also include data collection, translation, interpretation and even submission of the preliminary report. Indeed, referring to us as facilitating researchers is entirely appropriate given that we end up as the enabling link between the visiting researcher and the research outcomes. Some of us may never have an opportunity to complete any university education; however, we take great pride in the fact that researchers from top universities approach us to seek our knowledge. The researchers produce research based on what we have shared, revealed, and thus our knowledge gets widely circulated. Some of us who hold institutional positions or academic roles are advised to work on our own project rather than getting involved in someone's work, where we do not get paid adequately.

We differ from Sierra Leone regarding women working as facilitating researchers. In Jharkhand, India, both males and females serve as facilitating researchers depending on their knowledge of the area. Moreover, the number of females working as facilitating researchers exceeds the number of male counterparts. Both men and women are exposed to similar circumstances during fieldwork and undertake the same risks involved with the work. We come from different backgrounds and have chosen to work as facilitating researchers. We respect each other working as facilitating researchers, for we know how important it is to acknowledge someone's presence. Age has nothing to do with experience since our expertise and skills are developed through spending time in the field and developing a reliable network.

Generally, the researchers look for experienced facilitators; however, if they fail to find experienced hands, they choose the younger ones, but someone with proficiency in the local language and good local knowledge of the area. Nevertheless, in most cases, the selection of research facilitators is based on recommendations. The researchers know our potential capabilities before hiring us, yet they wish to keep us backstage. Most of us have offered all possible help to the researchers and have not sought any formal recognition for our work. However, one must also acknowledge that not everyone coming as a researcher is indifferent to our situation; they try to offer adequate and timely payment, are sympathetic to our struggles during fieldwork, and even after the project completion, they have continued to be in touch with us. Most of us do not have regular salaried employment so working on research projects is of great help, despite underpayment, overwork and lack of due recognition. One of our fellow research facilitators described the situation of working with research projects despite the exploitation as 'something is better than having nothing'.

Working with researchers from different countries does benefit us in terms of enrichment of knowledge. We have contributed to projects from prestigious global organizations like the UN. Affiliation with high-profile projects enriches our profile and potentially brings visibility to our work. We imagine that such an association may open other avenues for career progression. Some researchers have advised us to take up higher education, learn research methodologies, develop writing skills and pursue innovative research based on our first-hand knowledge. Our work with different projects has also inspired us to pursue formal research training, higher education and better language skills. Some of us feel constrained due to the lack of formal training and education and not having a university degree. On several occasions, we see ourselves as native informants, narrating our lived experiences, sharing our first-hand information, disclosing our traditional knowledge and imparting our privileged wisdom. No wonder we feel that while all the research is about us, the Adivasis and accomplished through us, we remain anonymous sources. We realize that the ongoing marginalization from the mainstream research is due to unequal power relations between the researchers and us. Some of us have also realized the need for higher education. It is a fact that formal recognition, institutional association and academic affiliation are necessary to gain visibility and ownership in knowledge production. One of us has shared her experience of becoming a facilitating researcher:

> *I was quite young then, a school going girl. One day I was standing and gossiping with my friends. Someone immediately approached us and asked us several things about the area. I was the one who provided him with all sorts of information. He happily handed me INR 3000, which was beyond my expectation. I had never imagined this in my life; this*

was quite surprising for me, just for a piece of information. The next time a different person handed me over INR 500 for the same work. Then gradually I realized that they are involved in some research projects funded by big institutions that need information. I came to know of my vital role in knowledge generation. Since then, I have readily engaged in such information sharing/provision for the money offered to me indeed helps me to run my household. Some have also helped in getting my work published, but I have also been cheated numerous times. I have also demanded greater remuneration for us as facilitating researchers. But the problem has not yet been sorted.

A leading Adivasi rights campaigner with outstanding credentials, comprehensive knowledge and significant work experience has ended up working as a research facilitator without even realizing it. She narrated that she had done exactly the kind of work the young and inexperienced research facilitators perform on numerous occasions. She described that she was not aware of the fact that she should receive remuneration or formal acknowledgement for all the work. Her long and prominent role in the movement for Adivasi rights has made her the cherished research partner for several researchers from India and abroad. She said:

I have spent hours and hours with them, answering their questions. I have taken them to the fields. I never denied anyone in the initial phase and went along with them. However, after complaints from the villagers, I have asked the researchers to visit themselves and then come to me for clarifications on what they observed. It is now that when I am talking to you, I am coming to know that you get paid for being a research facilitator. I became a facilitator because I felt good that so many people are interested in the Adivasis of Jharkhand. Moreover, I also wanted the other part of the world to know of the injustices done to Adivasis. My main aim was not monetary gain, so I never bothered about it. I cannot safely say each one of us thought the same way for there were few who did respond and did contribute to the movement.

Despite the known problems with the research projects, we realize that we look forward to employment in this work. However, unlike

Sierra Leone, we are not reliant on facilitating research work; most of us also have alternate employments. We derive a sense of pride that researchers make efforts to contact us and then we become part of the research project. We are quite willing to be a part of high-profile projects, even as part-timers. In recent times, given the commercialization of research and academic work, we have understood that several agencies have started to manage the supply chain of facilitating researchers. This business-like, transactional approach to research has further undermined our already limited agency and rendered us vulnerable and exposed to exploitation. The other chapters in the book examine the different forms of exploitation faced by facilitating researchers.

Reflections from the Eastern DR Congo: Facilitating research networks and the need to juggle various jobs

By Oscar Abedi Dunia, Elisée Cirhuza, Pascal Imili Kizee, Evariste Mahamba, Jérémie Mapatano, Lebon Mulimbi

As in the case of Sierra Leone, there are within us facilitating researchers at different levels. Most of the facilitating researchers in our (the bigger group of facilitating researchers writing in this book) have university degrees (bachelors and masters). Those who are connected to universities are PhD students or professors. But on a general level, there are also many facilitating researchers – some of whom are rather guides – with low educational levels. They can be close collaborators of armed groups that are active in the research area. They are used as facilitating researchers/guides for their local knowledge, the languages they speak, and because they are known by parts of the government army and by armed groups.

Almost all of our group members work not only as facilitating researchers within academic research, but also as facilitating researchers for NGOs and other actors of multi- or bilateral development cooperation (such as the UN). Sometimes we are also engaged as guides/translators/

facilitators by other actors, such as journalists. Actors within NGOs/ multi- or bilateral development cooperation generally offer more rigorous contracts where fees, insurance and other charges are taken into account compared to academic researchers and journalists. But the visibility of our work is also insufficient with these organizations, if not worse.

One of us manages a network of local facilitating researchers. It has a team of eight people and apart from research projects with universities in the West, this network also has contracts spread over several months with the above-mentioned kind of organizations. The leader of this network in our group is the one signing partnership protocols with the organizations or the international researcher/research team. He is usually asked to draw up the budget himself and propose it to them. Apart from this work, he manages a local organization and on an individual basis he sometimes facilitates foreign doctoral candidates, for instance. When he is hired by an academic researcher, he often does the fieldwork together with the person, sometimes accompanied by a team of people. If there is data to complete later, he sends out his team.

Many of us are part of this kind of locally managed networks. There are also those amongst us who, sometimes in addition to involvement in the network, are individually hired by foreign contracting researchers. But since engagements as research facilitator are sporadic and do not offer stable work, we must combine it with other occupations to survive, such as agriculture or the sale of merchandise. In some cases, these activities may provide opportunities to improve the network of contacts in a way that benefits the activities as facilitating researcher.

There are those amongst us who gave up their profession because it was difficult to combine ordinary activities with research projects. For example, being a study prefect is a role that is difficult to manage with regular absences of one or more week(s) caused by the commitments as facilitating researchers. At the same time, as developed in Chapter 5, the role of facilitating researcher does not ensure a stable income in the long run. However, the choice is difficult because local salaries are low compared to the cost of living which is constantly rising with the conflict. Therefore, the need for additional income is endless.

As research facilitators, we all regularly worked on sensitive topics, such as armed groups, peace processes, insecurity and land disputes. However, we also sometimes dealt with issues that are not directly linked to the conflicts, such as the education of girls as a human right. We carry out research activities in North Kivu in DR Congo and for some in the region of the Great Lakes. In these areas, a multitude of armed groups exist, who are very active and presumed perpetrators of serious human rights violations, often in the context of inter- and intra-ethnic conflicts.

The first time we were engaged in research happened through recommendations from other contracting researchers, like for our colleagues in Sierra Leone. For example, one of us explained that it was an old friend who recommended him to a foreign/contracting researcher. This happened at a time when he had lost his job and found himself in a complicated economic situation. For this first engagement, there was no contract or employment agreement, and it was only after two days in the field that the contracting researcher offered him a flat rate: $25 per day. Since he had no stable income and had already started working on the project, he had accepted.

3

The indispensable bridge: Without us no research

Oscar Abedi Dunia, Eric Batumike-Banyanga, Stanislas Bisimwa, John Ferekani Lulindi, Bienvenu Mukungilwa, Francine Mudunga, Lievin Mukingi and Darwin Rukanyaga Assumani

In this chapter, we will account for the various tasks that we perform as facilitating researchers, based mainly on the experiences of the researchers from the DR Congo. As we will show, in some ways the concept of 'facilitating' is not always enough, as so much of our work consists of tasks that could instead be seen as managing; managing/facilitating before, during, as well as after data collection. Importantly, the roles we play are much more varied and complex than what is stated in the contracts we work under – in the few cases we have clear and written contracts.

We chose the title 'indispensable bridge' as we occupy a position akin to a bridge – between contracting researchers coming from abroad and the research subjects. Since we live in or close to the data collection sites, we are the ones who have an understanding of the setting, are part of networks and have the necessary language skills, which make the research possible. In short, we are quite indispensable. Without us, much of research in the conflict-ridden eastern DR Congo would be impossible. Yet, as we will demonstrate in this chapter, living in the research settings where we work, our position also constitutes a major source of additional work even after the fieldwork has ended and the contracting researchers (if present at all during data collection) have left – work which is seldom recognized or remunerated.

While contracting researchers may not always understand this, we are the ones who become the 'outside face' of the research in relation to the local population. The contracting researchers are outsiders, often simply seen as another somewhat strange white person. Clearly, and as we will demonstrate, we can also be seen as 'outsiders' in different ways by the research subjects in different sites, through our backgrounds, ethnicities and educational status. Yet, compared to the contracting researchers, we still have an inside position; we know the language, culture, and traditions, and are seen as people who share or at least understand the difficulties of the local people. Moreover, if we are not trusted, the contracting researchers will also not be trusted. The trust that communities have in them, which can provide access to the field, depends on the trust research subjects have in us.

Clearly, research takes various forms. As such our roles also vary a bit depending on the project. A project involving a single researcher who engages one or two of us to accompany them to the field collecting limited data is quite different from large-scale projects involving several (teams of) facilitating researchers and sometimes also several contracting researchers (e.g. larger surveys or mapping exercises). Moreover, working with a contracting researcher who is new to the context is quite different from working with contracting researchers who have long-term experience from research in the eastern DR Congo and who may also master some Swahili. Yet, even if there is much variation, in this chapter we aim to provide a general picture of the various tasks performed by us.

Preparing access to the field

One of the tasks we perform – in case the contracting researcher is travelling to the eastern DR Congo to somehow accompany or oversee the research – is of course to plan for the arrival. Depending on who it is and what kind of research it is, this work can entail everything from assisting with paperwork for visas, booking hotels, arranging pick up at airports, renting cars and planning for pre-fieldwork workshops where a bigger group of facilitating researchers are to be instructed about the methodology of the research.

Yet, the most crucial preparatory work we conduct is to provide secure access to the field. It is important to note that this capacity is not something natural or inborn, already there. Clearly, not every citizen in the eastern DR Congo has the network or ability to ensure secure access to field sites. Rather it is a capacity that we have developed, and which also requires much work prior to the start of any research. Keeping in continuous touch with key actors and communities is crucial, not only in order to assess the necessary information, but also in order to create trust. Someone who only contacts you when she or he needs something – such as research access – is not seen as someone who can be trusted. Hence, having the capacity to make risk assessments and manage security is something that requires a lot of work and efforts before and after a particular research project. This is one aspect of the work we do that is not recognized as part of the research, neither in contracts nor remuneration. Yet, without this aspect, accessibility and security cannot be ensured.

Before continuing with more on the task of ensuring security and preparing access to the field, let us remind you about the environment of the eastern DR Congo (at the time of writing this book and since long before). While it varies from area to area and shifts over time, it is generally a highly volatile area with several armed groups, both foreign and domestic, operating. In addition, there are several criminal/bandit gangs that earn money from armed robberies and other activities. In recent years the kidnapping of people for ransom has also increased significantly. There are recurrent military operations and clashes between the Armed Forces of the State and various armed groups, creating insecurity and much injury and death in their wake. Moreover, inter-community tensions are high and also, at times fueled by politicians, seeking to increase their power and influence. Fast-evolving riots and popular justice mobs in which people are sentenced and punished – sometimes through death in public – without proper trials, are also recurrent.

A lack of vigilance in the face of all this can result in situations where researchers in a team are either injured in various ways, kidnapped or even killed. In order to get information in a rapidly changing security environment, we communicate with contacts in the setting we plan to conduct research, in order to make an assessment. We have several questions to ponder on and answer: Is this study really feasible in the location planned? How will we be seen bringing in strangers (i.e. contracting researchers) in the setting? Is there a risk that we may be suspected to be or bring in spies, by the security and intelligence services? If we are to carry out this study in a village where there has been a recent clash between armed groups and people are deeply traumatized, will they be able to answer the questionnaire brought by the contracting researchers? Is it even ethical to ask them? If we do, do we also have something to offer to them? Have the contracting researchers calculated for some small compensation to the people, we are likely to interview? In that case how much? Is it sufficient? If (which is sometimes the case) one of the aims of the research is to collect data on mass violent incidences (e.g. clashes, massacres, etc.), it becomes even more complicated. How will this be interpreted? How will we manage the risk of re-traumatization? How do we manage the expectations that we can somehow help these people more, directly? What about people who might still suffer injuries and need medical attention?

Hence, many questions are not simply about security issues, but ethical issues as well. Yet, by behaving in a way that is perceived as inhuman, by not offering assistance to people in need, there is also the risk of hostility and tension that may turn into a security risk. Managing expectations – which more concretely means trying to explain that we are researchers and therefore not able to give support – is often a tricky task, particularly given the presence of a white person. Even if we manage to explain that he/she is a researcher and not a humanitarian worker, he/she is still seen as someone with resources to help. In addition, by working with the white researchers, we as facilitating researchers become associated with resources and expectations to contribute. Depending on the contracting researcher (i.e. if she or he is willing to give or has provided some small compensation to the respondents or not) we often end up providing from our own pockets.

Once it has been decided that data-collection needs to be processed in a particular place, a lot of other preparations are needed. For example, there are safe hours and certain rules and precautions to be observed in areas of insecurity. Often time is a constraint, and a lot of data is to be collected in a number of villages under a tight schedule and one has to ensure that travelling to and from the location is done during day light, so there are many questions to answer: How is the road now between villages X and Y and how many road blocks will we pass? When do we have to leave village X in order to reach village Y before night fall? What if we run into problems with the car or are stopped at a newly installed roadblock? How much time should we allocate to unforeseen events like these?

In addition to the more general planning pertaining to the timing and security of travelling, there are several other arrangements. One crucial issue is to handle permissions and to arrange for meetings with local authorities in the chosen locations. A mission order document ('ordre de mission') containing the purpose of the visits, the institution responsible and in charge of the research, and the names of the places to be visited must be made. This must then be stamped and signed by the security officials in the bigger cities from where we often start the travel, for instance Goma, Bukavu or Uvira. Yet, this alone does not ensure safe and effortless travel and research, as it has to be shown to and signed by other authorities encountered on the way.

Moreover, plans have to be made to arrange meetings with various local authorities in the areas visited. Often several visits have to be scheduled to meet different authorities: state authorities, including security services, as well as traditional leaders. The nature of research partly influences the decision-making process when it comes to the person with whom the meeting has to be arranged and it is not always clear-cut. Hence, questions like these have to be addressed: Which authorities do we have to arrange meetings with, given the particular topic of the research and the locality? Whom can I ask to assist in introducing us and vouch for us in case I/we do not already have contacts with these people? Is it enough with this authority in this setting? In this particular setting where this person is newly instated, or might see us as suspicious and I have not yet established contact, what problems may I encounter? Or (for instance) in this particular setting, if the mayor tends to be difficult, will it be sufficient if we instead only seek audience with the security authorities?

Given the tight time schedules, we sometimes feel pressed to limit the number of official visits, even if it increases the risks. Moreover, especially contracting researchers with limited previous experience of the setting, sometimes do not understand the importance of these visits and appear to see them as unnecessary bureaucratic hurdles and a waste of time. Hence, in such situations we need to devote time to explain to them, or perhaps think once again if we still may be safe with a restricted number of meetings. In addition, and again mostly in relation to researchers with limited previous research experience in the eastern DR Congo, we also need to try to explain and guide in terms of appropriate behaviour during such meetings. Depending on the personality of the contracting researchers, this may be a bit delicate task. As we will describe in the chapter on security, some contracting researchers have a tendency to engage in suspicious and inappropriate behaviour putting the whole team at risk.

Moreover, official visits most often also involve costs: one often has to prepare to provide something for a successful outcome and continued trust and access. This can sometimes be difficult to explain for inexperienced contracting researchers and some are unwilling to pay anything. Sometimes contracting researchers calculate for such costs and provide them to us, since we are the ones who in turn give them to the official in question. But sometimes the money we get is not enough, the official complains that it is too little, exclaims for instance that 'you who work with these white people and get millions, the only thing you offer me is this?' Finally, depending on who it is and how important he/she is, very often we provide from our own pockets to resolve the issue. Sometimes, we haggle, say that this is what we have at the moment, and we will give more later. We seldom, unless it is a contracting researcher that we know will understand, tell them about this additional expense primarily to avoid any confrontation with them. Sometimes when we tell them, it seems like they do not believe us, think that we are trying to earn additional money for ourselves or perhaps think that we are bad negotiators.

In sum, we devote a lot of time and effort not just in relation to a specific research project – but also before and after the project – which includes planning and ensuring security. Yet, this is often not recognized in either contracts or remuneration, as we most of the times are simply paid for the days we are present in the field, collecting data (see Chapter 5).

Identifying respondents and preparing/adjusting research tools

In the previous section, we have accounted for the preparations related to security and risk that are particularly acute in insecure settings like ours. These tasks are thus added to the more 'normal' or 'expected' tasks of facilitating researchers, namely, to identify respondents, more specifically to locate them and adjust interview or questionnaire guides.

One important task that we do is preparing and adjusting the research tools, which most often come in the form of questionnaires or interview guides. This also includes the framing of the research project itself: What is the aim and how can we explain that in a manner that makes sense to the respondents? Most often, the contracting researcher comes with documents in French, so one task here is to translate it into Swahili. This is not an easy task as it is not just a matter of simple translation but also involves efforts for the questions to make sense and that they are easily understood by the respondents. The contracting researchers, naturally if they have limited experience of the context, often arrive with questionnaires or interview questions that are poorly suited to local conditions and understandings. Also, aims and questions that may be seen as rather innocent from the perspective of the contracting researchers may be interpreted in another way by the respondents in the setting, depending on the context and previous events. For instance, questions around land tenure and distribution, market regulations and trade may be very sensitive in some areas, but not in others. Sometimes, the aim and questions themselves are highly sensitive, for instance research on violence, the dynamics within and between armed groups or the state security forces or illegal activities. Such research requires extra work and preparation and is still conducted with great risk, not the least for us, and also after the data collection is over.

When the preparation, translation and adjustment of the research tools are completed, the task to identify the respondents remains. Since all research is different, the tasks here vary a lot. Some research aims to collect information from key-informants who – depending on the research aim – may be anyone from leaders of armed groups, traditional leaders, teachers, health workers, police officers or members of the armed forces. This kind of research has its own challenges when it comes to identifying the specific key-informants to the interview. Questions like: who do I/we know who can vouch for us and facilitate contact with the particular key-informant? Or who do I/we know who may know someone who – in turn can vouch for us to facilitate contact – with the particular key-informant? This task often involves a lot of thinking and calling upon the assistance of people in our networks.

Other, extensive research projects take the form of questionnaires or survey interviews with larger populations in an area. Also in such projects, identifying respondents and preparing for data collection are time-consuming. In addition to having all papers in order ('ordres de mission') and presenting these to the appropriate authorities in the location, a number of other questions need to be addressed: What is the appropriate location for the interviews? If the idea is to make it in the respondents' homes, this may be especially tricky as people tend to be out on various works and may not be at home during day-light when we need to conduct the interviews (due to security reasons, see previous section). Hence, often this is not possible, and we need to find other options instead.

Sometimes we choose the option of doing such surveys during market days arranged at different villages, as a lot of people from various walks of life can be reached out to, during such days. In these cases, after meetings with various authorities, including those responsible for the market, we identify respondents and conduct the interviews at the marketplace, in a more secluded space. In other cases, we ask our contacts in the villages to identify respondents who correspond to the profiles identified in the research and arrange for a place and time of the interviews. Whatever the option we decide to go for in relation to a specific research project, identifying respondents is a time-consuming work. In addition to calling up the different networks, it also often requires visits to the locations by ourselves before contracting researchers arrive in the country.

Collecting the data

At the core of what is defined as research (in addition to analysis and writing of course), is the data collection that we perform. Sometimes this is done together with the commissioning researcher. In those cases, often we have also been engaged in other practical issues related to his/her arrival, such as booking hotels, arranging for pick-up at airport, invitation letters for visas, etc. (see the previous section). Yet sometimes we go to the field alone and the contracting researchers are either still in Europe/United States, or stay on in the bigger cities like Goma and Bukavu.

Why they do not always accompany us to the field surely has various reasons. Sometimes, we sense that they fear the risks involved in the travel and decide against it. Sometimes, we judge that it is too risky both for them and for us to bring them to the field, particularly as white people are more vulnerable to be suspected to be spies. Yet, and as described in the Introduction, there has also been an increasing securitization and regulation of field visits in Europe and the US. In short, the contracting researchers are sometimes not allowed to leave the safer bigger cities like Goma and Bukavu. Hence, if they travel anyway, they will not be covered by their insurance. Clearly, we have no insurance and limited attention is directed to questions regarding what will be done if we are victims of events that may require financial resources. More details on that theme will be developed further in Chapter 5 focusing on security.

Hence, often we go to the field on our own, with instructions from the contracting researcher who stay on in a safe place in Europe or the United States or at a nice hotel in Goma and Bukavu. We are often under tight schedules in the field as we have a deadline when we are to be back and report on the data collection and findings. Sometimes we are also sent to the field to collect supplementary data after the main data collection has been completed.

When we collect data on our own, contracted by others, we travel and live in fairly humble circumstances. The budget for our travels and accommodations is often quite low – and different from that of the contracting researcher. Moreover, since our remuneration in general is low and we often have to cover various contributions to key gate keepers and research subjects from our own pockets. Sometimes we also deliberately choose the cheapest transport or even walk on foot, in order to save some money.

When contracting researchers join the data collection process, the situation is quite different. While we sometimes stay in the same places in the villages (i.e. small hostels), since the availability of comfortable accommodation is rather limited, the travelling is often vastly different. Some contracting researchers like PhD students with smaller projects and more limited budgets can travel on motorbikes or use public transportation; while accompanying a senior contracting researcher in the field/ for data collection often means travelling by a hired car. Therefore, one of the tasks we do in such cases is to arrange for a car on rent and a driver before the arrival of the contracting researcher, something that can sometimes take time and involve negotiations around rates and responsibilities in case of damage, as we often have to hire from private persons or NGOs.

During field visits (as well as before) we act as translators when contracting researchers conduct interviews themselves. However, we also devote quite a lot of time and effort to try to inform the contracting researchers about culture and traditions in the location, especially when it comes to researchers not familiar with the site. This includes, for instance, how to greet and approach authorities in the location, where we generally are the ones expected to talk and introduce the research and the researcher (rather than the contracting researcher taking the lead, which may cause suspicion). It also includes explaining other traditions that shape the methods chosen. For instance, sometimes the contracting researchers want to conduct group interviews with mixed groups. Yet, in some locations this is not seen as appropriate to mix women and men with particular family relations in the same group or mix people with different ethnic backgrounds. Hence, we are the ones who have to take responsibility for the research being conducted in a spirit which does not abuse community customs and traditions. Depending on the personality of the contracting researcher, playing this role is not always easy. While some are eager to learn and happy to take a back seat position, others seem to find it more difficult, in turn making our position as a bridge arduous.

Additionally, data collection poses a lot of other challenges and tasks, pertaining to security and which becomes particularly difficult given the tight time schedules. A lot of data is to be collected during a very limited time, in difficult circumstances. As people naturally are busy with their own lives and making a living, interviews seldom start according to schedule as people do not arrive as per the anticipated timings. This, in turn, leads to delays and new sets of questions such as: maybe we need to drop some of the planned interviews in order to be able to leave at a safe hour? Should we come back tomorrow instead? Or even, could we start this group interview even if not all have arrived yet? Given the present composition with some people missing, will it still be valuable to the research?

Yet, it should be emphasized that we do not only collect data in concert to these kind of visits to the field as mentioned previously. Sometimes we are also hired on a more ad hoc basis. For instance, a contracting researcher in Europe or the United States may contact us and ask 'can you go to this location and collect this kind of data and send to us'? Hence, in these cases we are picked up halfway in a project we know nothing about. If you are asked to work on an iPad, these are directly connected to the server somewhere in Europe or the United States. Once you have completed your data collection in the evening, you click 'send' and the data is sent to the computer of the contracting researcher located somewhere else.

Interpretation and translation of collected data

We also assume a lot of responsibility in terms of interpretation and translation of the collected data. Since the contracting researcher does often not master Swahili, we not only have to translate the aims and interview or questionnaire questions, but also the responses and make a preliminary analysis. Sometimes this work is included in the contract, but most often it is not, as it is expected to be done at the end of each day in the field.

Often, we are asked to summarize the data collected by the end of each day, even if the contracting researcher was present herself/himself. We are asked to present the general findings and give our interpretations as well as how that should guide the data collection the next day. Clearly, such practices and daily debriefing are good, but in addition to all our other work during the day (conducting interviews, ensuring that people turn up for interviews, managing expectations and security concerns, etc.), they also wear heavy on us by the end of a tiresome day. Sometimes, we also wonder what the point is for the contracting researcher to go into the field in the first instance, if he/she still asks us to provide so many details?

In short, we do a lot of work in terms of summarizing the data collected and provide our understandings of how the data could be interpreted, given our understanding of the context and the actors interviewed. For instance, how can we interpret accounts of actors and actions during an incidence of mass violence? Who were the people interviewed and what position do they have in relation to ongoing tensions and conflicts? Do they have particular reasons to name a particular actor as the perpetrator? How can we corroborate the data? Who are the other people we need to consult? It is only through our profound knowledge of shifting dynamics and positionality of respondents that such questions can get informed answers.

In other cases, we provide important cultural interpretations of the data collected, particularly when concerning more sensitive issues. Moreover, and importantly, we are able to observe much more during field research. While contracting researchers tend to be restricted by what is said in interviews, we are often able to observe and detect other events. We can often more easily, by observing the environment and the reactions of other people around, detect when people are not truthful and sometimes people also approach us in secret during fieldwork to provide additional information about key-informants. In this way, we can sometimes provide more accurate data on, for instance, power relations, shifting support and allegiances for particular leaders, levels of wealth and sources of income, including illegal activities. Without such data, many projects would produce quite accommodated and incorrect answers to the research questions posed. Hence, our capacity and contribution here are very important for the quality of the data and research.

In short, we have a crucial role in contributing to informed and reliable research results. One of us summarized it in a good way, saying that 'even if we may not have a doctorate in medicine or any other area of expertise where we collect data, we are doctors in our understanding and mastery of the area of research'.

During fieldwork we are also often asked to provide our ideas on new research plans that the contracting researchers are planning and help in identifying new possible fields of study. Yet, our participation often ends with the process of summarizing and interpreting the data. As this is subject of a chapter of its own, we will not dwell much on it here. Yet, we would still like to emphasize that many of us are highly frustrated by not being offered the opportunity to be listed as co-authors, a theme developed on in the next chapter. Often, we are told that the reason is that we have not contributed to the writing of the text. But how can we contribute to a process we are not invited to? Moreover, does the crucial role we play in designing the research, collecting and interpreting data not merit co-authorship?

Managing the after-work of fieldwork

However, and as alluded to in the Introduction, our work is not over when we have finished the data collection and assisted in interpreting the data. While we are seldom invited to be part of the writing or appear as co-authors, we – in addition to being asked questions of interpretation or being asked to collect complementary data – have to answer questions and problems that may arise in the wake of data collection. We are the ones who, often in relation to subsequent research, have to answer the questions from the population: 'What happened with the research? What are the results? When and how will it help us?'

There is a growing fatigue in our locations of all the researchers who come to take information without any visible positive impact for the people who are asked to contribute with their time. In short, there is an increasing research fatigue in the communities, which also makes it more and more difficult to get people to participate in research. A common reaction when we prepare for new data collection is: 'Your colleagues were here the day before yesterday. My brother, I don't have time, I have to go and do my business.'

Moreover, and as emphasized before, even if fieldwork for one project is over, we need to nurture our networks in order for them to be present for the next project. This is both a time- and money-consuming activity. You need to keep and nurture the contacts in various ways, by calling, buying a beer from time to time, etc. As highlighted initially, being able to provide secure access to field sites requires staying in contact with relevant and key actors in between the research projects we are involved in. Access and continued good relations depends on reciprocity and continued contact. You cannot stay away and only approach people when you yourself are in need of a favour again.

A lot of requests for compensation for facilitating research also arrive after fieldwork has ended, questions/requests like: 'I am in some trouble, I would need some support' – with the implicit unsaid 'You remember how I helped you in facilitating contacts during that fieldwork you did with those white people?'. Sometimes, as described above we were also not able to provide the expected compensation for facilitation during the research and we end up in a debt that we are expected to pay in some way or another.

Sometimes we also have to manage unforeseen consequences of research that affect our security. Sometimes the security problems arise after data collection is complete, when the contracting researchers have left. It is sometimes then that we are approached by security authorities accusing us for 'bringing in spies from the outside'. Or for being unpatriotic and 'dragging the name of the country in the dirt' by assisting in research on issues like sexual violence or illegal mineral extraction. We will provide more examples of this in the chapter on security.

Reflections from Jharkhand, India: Managing bureaucratic hurdles and working under extreme stress in risky situations

By Anju Oseema Maria Toppo

Our experiences as research facilitators in India are not too different from the DR Congo team, and we too consider ourselves the indispensable bridge to the promised land of distinguished research.

However, as exemplified in the chapter, sharing the glory of successful research with those who form the indispensable bridge remains 'a bridge too far'. As we will elaborate more in the next chapter, in the initial phases of the project, the visiting researchers often offer an enriching and fruitful engagement with the local research facilitators. However, upon the completion of the project, the same researchers often either express their incapacity in attributing the due recognition or go incommunicado altogether.

Similar to the experiences of our DR Congo colleagues, we know that external researchers will not be able to make sense of the actual situation without our assistance. Everything these visiting researchers find in the books/journals is mostly an outsider perspective and can be quite different from ground realities. The literature from the indigenous scholars and activists is largely marginalized from the mainstream; the researchers require our help to bring such indigenous knowledge production to their notice.

Some researchers from foreign lands try to learn Hindi before visiting the areas, but this is not a great help. Field subjects speak their mother tongue like *Kurukh, Mundari, Santali*, which the researcher fails to understand. In these times, we are of great help, and they have no choice other than to put their faith in us. The researchers brief us on the research and what they want; the rest is framing the questions. The outcome of such interviews is such which the researcher could have never expected. Language brings people close to each other; they may communicate in Hindi but will not develop a close link with the subjects as we do and get the required information.

In the Adivasi populated areas of Jharkhand (India), some places are quite sensitive given the ongoing Naxalite movement and the strained relations between the Adivasis and the state security forces. Several of these conflict areas cannot be accessed by everyone and are certainly not safe for outsiders. It is quite dangerous even for us to enter these areas, for we are sometimes suspected of helping the Naxalites and face harassment from the state security forces. Moreover, most of the villagers also suspect us, seeing us as state agents. We literally risk our lives to provide the researchers with secure access to fieldwork and find answers to their investigations. While some of the researchers are indeed grateful for our endeavours, a large number of them do not consider our high-risk enterprise as worthy of due recognition or adequate compensation.

Akin to our DR Congo colleagues, we have to go through several bureaucratic hurdles and undergo several procedures to enter the fields. Beyond the official red tape, we need to get written permission from the village assembly and village headmen. It is a lengthy process; we need to prove that the visitors are bona fide researchers and not enemies of the villagers. The local research facilitators need to have proper contacts, existing affiliation and some form of recognition among the people to facilitate such approvals for visiting researchers. However, we feel that the contracting researchers do not appear to appreciate the efforts required to nurture and sustain such tenuous links between us, the local research facilitators and the local people.

There are times when we feel let down by the cavalier attitude of the researchers. And as highlighted by our colleagues in the DR Congo, we are also often very stressed because the researchers sometimes act as if we have no value. One of us had the following experience when facilitating a research project:

> *They want everything to be served to them without delay. They try to show that their time is very important, and we are wasting it. Once it so happened that the car driver got late, he had to rush to the hospital with his daughter who had high fever. But even after knowing this, the researcher was so insensitive that she started scolding him. This is not humane. It seems that they just come in search of answers for their questions.*

In Jharkhand, India, we neither book hotels for the researchers nor arrange for their visas and transportation. However, sometimes the researchers wish to visit the field and insist on staying there for a few days, then we have to arrange for their stay in the local community. Villagers are often very welcoming, especially when they know that a foreigner will stay in their house. People always see them with respect; it also allows them to brag about hosting overseas visitors.

Accordingly, such a high-profile visitor is offered the best possible hospitality without any recompense by all the family members. However, it is disappointing to find that on many occasions, the visiting researchers do not feel gratitude for their care and leave without even thanking the host family. We feel bad to hear such things and feel responsible for such inconsiderate behaviour. It makes things difficult for us to sustain our rapport with the local villagers, for they might think that we, the research facilitators, received money for the food and lodging from the visiting researcher, and we have kept the money to ourselves.

Sometimes the researchers have limited time to offer in the field, and so the work remains incomplete. We then make frequent visits to the field and send all the data and reports to the researchers in these situations. While the mails and phone calls are quite frequent during the data gathering phase, once the data collection is over, it is hard to get in touch with the researchers.

Most of us doing PhD are also told not to publish anything out of this work until the report gets released. We are not supposed to use the data for our works without the permission of the contracting researcher. We wait because we consider ourselves as a part of the research project. We want to see our names included in the publication, for we know we played a vital role in its completion. We mark ourselves everywhere and are not just limited to data collection.

Reflections from Sierra Leone: The importance of knowing the right language and traditions and the difficulties in managing expectations and keeping good report

By James B Vincent

We recognize most aspects which the DR Congo team draws attention to in this chapter. Although with a variety of facilitating roles, a constant factor for us is that contracting researchers come and go, even though some have long-term commitments, and we live and continuously work in the very research environment.

As highlighted by our DR Congo colleagues, maintaining good rapport, protecting our respectable names and our correct moral behaviour are pivotal for not just the success of work, but to be able to live and reside in our communities not just for us, but for our close and extended families. We are the guarantors in the face of the local communities that the 'stranger/white person', but also the urban-based Sierra Leonean researcher/consultant (see Chapter 6), is not there to do harm. We also truly recognize the rather impossible role to manage expectations. As one of us concluded during the workshop:

> *In the villages they get perceptions of white people. White people have money. They have power. They think that white people are more intelligent than black. They feel proud if a white person shake [sic] their hands, play with their children. It is like if a minister comes from Freetown. It is the same level. And they always feel it is help they come to give. That's like one of us stated yesterday, there are places where it is hard to go back. Because they think we have something to give them. And they will always say to us that we should try to get help from the researcher. That's why if you go with a smart researcher, it is good. If you come with a researcher without money and you don't give them anything, or just something small, they think that you have taken the money and hidden it for them.*

We all agree with this, and several of us avoid certain areas, villages or communities where we have previously carried out work, but in the eyes of the local community failed to deliver.

Another issue highlighted by the DR Congo team worth underscoring is that we know the language, culture and traditions. It is indeed a key asset. However, we want to reiterate how important it is to know the right language, or the traditions of a particular area. It is culturally an advantage of being a Sierra Leonean, but we quite frequently work with Sierra Leoneans who are born and raised in the capital. They too may not know the local language, and although they understand the ins and outs of our culture better, they often fail to see this lacuna. As one of us concluded during the workshop: '*From my perspective, a local researcher who has not been to a particular area is equal to the international researcher. If you are from Freetown and you have never been to Kailahun, what's the difference?'* From our experience it is an invaluable asset to have a facilitator who works in the language of the area. Working with so many different researchers, another point we agree upon is how important it is if the contracting researcher makes an effort to learn a local language. Even a few greeting phrases make a great difference.

A difference we found between DR Congo and Sierra Leone is the question of written clearances. If we look back at experiences from the war, we rarely travelled with formal mission order documents. In some ways, it made travelling easier as there was less paperwork beforehand, but in other ways, it also became more hazardous. Successful travel often depended on who operated the checkpoints when we intended to pass. We very much relied on personal contacts in a time when movement of staff was rapid or hard to foresee. Some of us became known to rebel soldiers and army alike because we constantly travelled up and down the same road. They recognized our faces or in one instance even our car which stuck out because of its colour. That made travel easier, but on the other hand if we, or the researcher we travelled with, did something wrong we could not hide. Largely, we depended on informal clearances and personal contacts rather than mission order documents.

Another difference from DR Congo and this may depend on the fact that the civil war in our country ended a rather long time ago, was that we rarely carried out field studies without the contracting researcher. They were with us in the field. Quite often we travelled on motorbikes, in shared taxis, and lived under the same simple conditions as we did. Researchers we work with today continue to go to the field and are present most of the times when we carry out work, but then again Sierra Leone is now a conflict-free and rather low-risk country.

4

Systematically silenced and non-recognized

Anju Oseema Maria Toppo

Some amongst us have never received any remuneration for offering help, assistance and guidance, and even to this day hesitate to accept any remuneration for sharing our time, knowledge and experiences with contracting researchers. This is despite the fact that most researchers would not even care to send us a copy of their published pieces, whose data, analysis and most of the findings are based on our information. It is quite clear that while the research on Jharkhand and our assistance may have helped the researchers attain an educational degree, an academic milestone, or a career progression, the Adivasis[1]' life remains the same.

It is a known fact that for any social, cultural, economic or political research in Jharkhand (India), the bulk of available data collection is performed or accomplished through us, the local Adivasis. Although the data is collected by us, the locally based facilitating researchers, and serves as one of the most critical parts of the research process, our role often goes unacknowledged. In Chapter 3, we described the various tasks that we perform as facilitating researchers. While we

---

[1] The term 'Adivasi' refers to the indigenous population of India. The original inhabitants who have been residing in the land since ages, tribals of the mainland are popularly referred to as Adivasis. The Adivasi communities have been named as 'Scheduled Tribes' (STs) in the Indian constitution to provide them with protection and rights.

have already mentioned about the lack of visible acknowledgement for our research contributions, the core theme of this chapter is lack of recognition and silencing, written from the perspective of Jharkhand, India, with additional reflections from the DR Congo and Sierra Leone at the end.

Since the aim is to capture not just my own experience, the chapter is written in a 'we' form. We start the chapter with some reflections on the various reasons for our involvement in facilitating research and also how that differs between us; because experiences of silencing and non-recognition, of course, not only depend on the promises made by contracting researchers, and how these are often broken (as we will demonstrate in this chapter), but also on the various reasons why we engage in such work. Next, we elaborate on the various promises that are often made to us and are subsequently broken, in relation to contracting researchers and ourselves, such as disappearance/lack of feedback, broken promises about remuneration, co-authorship and job/study opportunities. In the following part we elaborate on what could be described as 'broken promises' in relation to the research subjects. Clearly, the lack of concern and respect for research subjects also affects us, as discussed by the DR Congo team in Chapter 5, and we think it is important to put them at the forefront and, therefore, organize the chapter in this manner. We conclude by discussing our apprehensions and experiences of not being able to voice our thoughts on the same to our contracting researchers.

The various reasons why we engage

Let us start by reminding the reader of the context of Jharkhand, a site where the abundance of, and quest for, natural resources have time and again led to fierce resistance from the local Adivasis, who try to protect their land, natural resources, and distinct cultural and social milieu. In the last few decades, this resistance has manifested itself in movements such as the Naxalite[2] and *Patthalgari*.[3] These resistance movements have particularly drawn worldwide research attention.

The accounts of experiences in this chapter are, in addition to my own experience, based on a diverse set of people, who like me facilitate research. As described in the Introduction chapter, workshops similar to those in the DR Congo and Sierra Leone could not be held in Jharkhand due to the pandemic. Instead, I conducted informal interviews with co-facilitating researchers. While some of the colleagues interviewed are PhD students like myself, we have also included teachers, government employees, social and NGO activists. Three prominent Adivasi activists – Dayamani Barla, Barkha Lakra and Aloka Kujur – have made immense contributions to the research done on Jharkhand. They have played vital role in most of the movements seeking Adivasi rights and despite their busy schedules have always found the time to help researchers and knowledge seekers. These three, like myself, are women and also specifically involved in work related to gender equality and women's rights. While we have participated in a range of research projects, covering various topics, we have mainly participated in projects related to the positioning of Adivasi women in the society, their empowerment in Jharkhand, Adivasi women's relationship with the environment, migration, housing rights, ownership rights, mining, displacements, informal settlements, etc.

---

[2] The Naxalite movement is widely and popularly spread in the Adivasi populated areas of India and takes its name from Naxalbari in Bengal, where it all started. The Naxalites have led an armed resistance against the oppression and harassment of the Indian State since the 1970s. Seeing Indian Democracy as a sham, they have challenged this institution to bring in, what they see as real democracy and sovereignty. The Naxalities believe in overthrowing the existing state and largely draw their cadres from the Adivasi communities. The state has always brutally suppressed the Naxalite movement, and in pursuing its counter insurgency operations it has come to target several innocent Adivasis who have no connection with the movement.

[3] The *Patthalgari* movement was a resistance movement led by Adivasis of Jharkhand against who they perceived as 'outsiders' and the forces of the state. Through the movement the Adivasis tried to assert their right over *Jal, Jungle* and *Zameen* (water, forest and land) by erecting stone slabs at their village entrances, and carving the autonomy of the Gram Sabhas under the Fifth Schedule of the Indian Constitution.

Clearly, our motivation for participating as facilitating researchers can differ. For doctoral students and teachers, getting academic credit for the work done is particularly important. For advancement in our academic careers, the research work that we do needs to be recognized and given due credit. We realize that being asked to participate in prestigious research or work with an eminent researcher is important for our growth and academic careers. Though we wish to be named as co-authors for our work, most of the times, the contracting researcher remains the sole author.

Yet, even for those who do not aspire for an academic career, some kind of recognition other than remuneration is of course important. One of the most overriding desires to engage in the work we do is to derive a sense of recognition of our knowledge/expertise, whatever form that may take. Moreover, what all of us also share is a concern for indigenous rights and empowerment. At significant risk and discomfort, we take the researchers to some of the most inaccessible parts of Jharkhand to get a firsthand experience of the trials and tribulations endured by the Adivasis on a daily basis. Yet, as we describe below, our work is not recognized and contracting researchers often show little respect for our communities, culture and our struggles.

Moreover, many of us who are social and political activists, envision our role in the research project as an extension of our work as activists. We gravitate towards research projects that purportedly focus on certain social or cultural issues which we tend to identify with, as part of our social and political agenda for change. Some of us come as dedicated social activists, and we consider our affiliation with the research project as an opportunity to broaden our engagement and intellectual horizons with social issues like displacement, environment, gender and Adivasi history.

Hence, most of us do not participate in a project only for money. We almost never negotiate or quibble over money and as reflected in the initial citation some of us are even least bothered, as we have other occupations that remain our sustainable sources of income. Few amongst us were not even aware that one gets paid for sharing information. Yet, our situations in terms of livelihood opportunities differ and for some of us the expectation of additional income is an incentive as it is not easy to find well-paid long-term work. Yet, as we account for below, broken promises by contracting researchers also sometimes include remuneration. We have come across several instances during our work that would be seen as unethical behaviour, prejudices, underpayment, denial of due recognition for scholarly work and several forms of exploitation. One among us summed it up well during the interview,

> *What! One gets paid for narrating experiences or sharing any sort of details? I am coming to know of this for the first time. Are you serious? (laughs). There are so many who come to me seeking help in their research. And I talk to them for hours and hours. I give them all possible help by providing them information. But so far nobody has offered me any monetary compensation. You are the first person to tell me of this.*

Broken promises: Absence of feedback, job/work opportunities and remuneration

We would like to start by mentioning that we have noticed greater attempts towards implementing diversity and inclusivity in hiring research staff over the years. Since much social science research focuses on marginalized communities especially in our setting, it is a suitable policy to adopt, whether formal or informal. Unfortunately, much of this new trend of hiring people from diverse backgrounds is a race to the bottom, offering the low paid, tedious and most menial of intellectual work.

The new jobs offered to us mainly include work as field workers or research assistants with little to no control over the decision-making process and practically no input to the conduct of the research process. We receive very little information about the projects that we engage in and are seldom asked to provide substantial inputs. Hence, most of us have no clear idea of the project we are working on, for we are only provided details of what the contracting researcher wants. If the project is on sexual violence, we are sent to women police stations and grievance cells to collect data on such cases. Once the data collection is completed, we are asked to submit a hard copy of the reports. Then it seems our role is over. When we sometimes try to get in contact with the contracting professors, they often reject our telephone calls. We then realize that all the promises made to us were fake, and unknowingly we have helped the contracting researcher to get his/her work done. We are quite sure that the contracting researcher might have published our findings in his/her name. One of us shared the following experience,

> *I was looking for an advisor for more than eight months and eventually my search ended when a professor working in a prestigious institution in Ranchi assured me. When I paid him a visit with my synopsis he rejected it and asked me to work on a different topic which was related to female prisoners. He briefed me about everything i.e. from where I can collect data, whom I have to interview, which books I have to review etc. He gave me a month's time to complete this task and then submit the complete report. In the meantime, I kept on persuading him to begin my enrolment process for the PhD programme but in vain for he said that he will consider me only after I submit this report. He used to call me up twice in a week to check the work progress. Finally, I met him after a month to submit the report. He acted very friendly, made me submit every piece of information and told me that he will speak to me of the enrolment over the phone. But since then, every time I used to call him, he would disconnect my call and finally blocked my number. Once I visited him but he showed up to be very busy and finally left saying no to me. One day while I was scrolling through some articles, I found an article of this person which was actually not his but completely mine. I came to know that he was working on a project related to this. This was my first experience of this kind. I was shocked to find the ugly truth that most respectable big shots in the academia can do this.*

Indeed, our engagement is indispensable to the project's success given our ability to collect accurate and rich data based on our networks, perceptive insights about the field and the ability to inhabit the research subjects' life-world. However, despite having local knowledge and working as a bridge between the research subjects and the researcher, we face mistreatment, low pay and heavy workloads. Ironically, these unethical practices occur frequently, although contracting researchers would find it nearly impossible to research without our support. We have assessed that high-profile projects involving some of the most prestigious institutions that aim to study and address marginalization, exclusion and exploitation of disadvantaged communities perpetuate the same marginalization, exclusion and exploitation of underprivileged facilitating researchers.

Before commencing the fieldwork for projects, there are often many kinds of promises made. Contracting researchers often promise us a handsome remuneration, a copy of the journal and the book where potentially this research would be published. Sometimes co-authorship is also promised or job or study opportunities. Yet, this is not what happens. Instead, a common experience is that of disappearance. One of us describing her experience said:

> *A lady had come from America to work on a project which was on the empowerment of women. I took her to several places, introduced her to several local tribal women and also provided her my materials on tribal way of life. After she left, I had no clue where she disappeared, may be flew away or went under the ground! Neither did I receive any proper remuneration for my work, nor do I have any idea of what and where she published. There was another lady who was an Indian but had come from Malaysia to research on Adivasi culture. I had taken her to villages for her understanding of the parha panchayat, also to the village of Birsa Munda and Gaya Munda. They [sic] did promise of a documentary film which would be circulated widely. But there was nothing that I heard off after they disappeared.*

Such disappearance is not always the case. On completing data collection, some researchers sometimes return and call us a couple of times and sometimes send us follow-up emails to enquire about more details or information related to their fieldwork. However, after a few days, there are often no follow-up contacts. Even when we make multiple attempts to reach the overseas researcher by phone or email, it goes unanswered. To this day, most of us do not know the research outcomes, potential publications or any other subsequent developments emerging from the research we have engaged in. Hence, many of us have had several rather disappointing experiences when most of the researchers disappeared despite the pledges of maintaining a long-term association. On their return from the fieldwork in Jharkhand, researchers promise to be in touch with us, but they seldom return or respond to our emails. '*Copy kalam band karne ke baad koi lautkar nahi ata*' (nobody returns after closing the notebook and keeping the pen aside) was something that was constantly repeated in our discussions about our experiences.

This experience of disappearance is general and also includes those of us who are PhD scholars. We often get involved in the research projects with no benefits from the other end. We get an opportunity to become part of the project through known sources or early associations. We are happy to align with the project of our interest because we want to have a learning experience. Hence, we get involved in the fieldwork, data collection, data entry and preparation of preliminary reports. Initially, we are promised multiple outcomes like handsome remuneration and experience certificates. However, promises turn out to be vague, and we find that the final arrangement is very different from the initial one. We are often not even given access to the final report for which we had put in a lot of effort to collect the data. We also come to know of major conferences being organized in India and abroad wherein we are not invited. We never get a chance to meet the people at the other end, and if we want to glance at our own collected data, we are made to run around.

It is a rarest of the rare thing to see ourselves projected as a co-authors, mostly we do not get this opportunity. Even if there is any sort of grievance from our end, we do not know whom to contact. During the course of research, some amongst us who had an idea about the source of the project tried to complain about the mismanagement on the part of the contracting researcher. But unfortunately, several allegations were levied against them by the contracting researcher, and they were also pushed out of the project. One of us shared her previous experience with the contracting researcher:

> Two of us were working for a contracting researcher. I was closely working with the field worker and was also into writing the final draft of the research project. I felt the field worker's condition was far worse than me. He was a rickshaw driver and depended on the project for income too. But the researcher had not paid him the amount for travel and other expenses as committed. He was underpaid and even mistreated, for his English was weak. So, the field worker finally decided to complain and send an email to the director. When the contracting researcher was questioned of this, she completely denied and undertook the responsibility of investigating herself. One fine day I got [sic] a long email from the researcher in which she mentioned the kind of accusation the field worker has made and also reported that the data had been [sic] mismanaged, and falsified. She said for some reason she feels that the one who has complained has trust in me and wants to add me everywhere. So, is it me who asked him to falsify the data? I was so shocked to hear this. To save her face she accused me of all these things. I learnt a lot from this incident and I keep a record and screenshots of all the chats and messages. Often it is the research assistants who are blamed.

As reflected above, broken promises also entail remuneration. There are so many of us who have been promised handsome remuneration at the end of the month. Never do we daydream of the amount, nor negotiate; we are actually informed about the amount we would be receiving for facilitating research. However, in most cases promises never turn out to be realities. The package promised for an entire month turns out to be misleading. Instead of paying fixed emoluments our payment is based on number of persons we have interviewed in the month. Some of us have also been asked about our hourly input in the research per day and we are paid as per the calculation of the researcher. Most of us have witnessed that when we are made to sign the receipts against the payment made, the amount mentioned is higher than what they have given us. This brings the ongoing corruption to our knowledge. The receipt signed by us is kept for the records by the researcher to show the facilitators have not been exploited financially during the course of the research work and that he/she has utilized every single penny in carrying out the project. But in reality, the researchers do not reimburse the logistics and other travel expenses.

Another broken promise that we often experience is the lack of information and sudden unexpected changes in our work. At times, after delivering a significant portion of our assignments, suddenly and without any discussion, we are transferred to another project. The researchers make no formal negotiations or revisions in the contract, and even working conditions remain the same. The projects oblige us to shoulder more significant responsibilities; the work scope also increases substantially; there is no corresponding increase in our work profile or remuneration. One amongst us shared her bitter experience of how she was overburdened with work:

> *The researcher with whom I was working was not able to manage and retain people. I had joined her to do one study but even before it was [sic] ended properly, I was asked to do another. There was lot of work, everything got dumped on me. I knew I am being exploited. But I had salary with the project and was treated with dignity, so I continued with the project. The researcher should have paid me more since I was looking into two projects.*

Broken promises in relation to the local community

As concluded initially, we are not the only ones experiencing broken promises. The same applies to the research subjects: at first many promises are made. Most visiting researchers claim to forge a long-term and fruitful association with our social, political and cultural activism, promising support for these movements. Yet, we have undergone much sobering experiences, as many contracting researchers appear to lack genuine compassion for the hardships of the Adivasis. Instead, it seems they are only keen to extract maximum information about everything related to the Adivasis to use and advance their own careers.

At times, we regret introducing the villagers to the overseas researchers. If we introduce someone to the local communities, the Adivasi women warmly welcome the researcher to the village by washing his/her feet, an honour of exceptional order in the Adivasi community. Sometimes, we request some locals, both males and females, to accompany the researcher as per the researcher's wish. They leave behind their work on the farm, which is their only source of income. However, the researcher seldom pays these men and women for their labour. Moreover, as described in Chapter 3, we sometimes arrange for contracting researchers to stay with the local community and they are always well received, offered the best possible hospitality. Yet, as concluded in that chapter some leave without any gift, not even sweets for the children as a token of appreciation. One of us, sharing his nasty experience with researchers, said, *'They know just one thing, operate the camera, click pictures and switch on the voice recorder. I have encountered few who were mannerless, insensitive and short tempered.'*

As facilitating researchers, we realize that the researchers who do not understand the local customs, norms and social etiquettes tend to hide their ignorance through arrogance. These researchers would tend to become very dominant; they would try to dictate terms, remarkably some would even dare to berate people in the community. On the other hand, villagers remain curious about the researchers and tend to believe that their intervention would lessen their hardships and deliver some benefits to them. They, like us, see the promises of potential publication or a documentary film, as an opportunity to share their life stories and precarious existence with a broader audience that eventually may bring some relief. However, on most occasions, such promised documentaries never get out of the researcher's camera, and all of us end up wasting our time, energy and emotions.

Similar to what our DR Congo colleagues point out in Chapter 5, it seems contracting researchers lack humanism and empathy for the communities, who often live with extremely limited means. Time and again, they come to ask questions about poverty, like 'how much and what is your source of income?' The research subjects feel delighted to answer them. They open their hearts, sometimes expecting some help from the other end. However, neither do they receive any direct help, nor do these researchers do anything to draw attention to their plight. In the words of one of us:

> *There are so many cases filed against the Adivasis, so many court cases going on, so many Adivasis have been killed in encounters and are blamed of being Naxalites, so many women facing several injustices. But what has been done by these researchers who just show their compassion in the fields. What we require is practical help and what they need is our stories.*

We feel guilty that we have lied to the people and misused their trust and courtesy on an unethical adventure. It is primarily because of the contracting researchers that we feel betrayed. We regret being part of such exploitative projects, which take so much free labour from many of us without any material, intellectual or emotional recompense. Initially, we were quite happy to take the researchers to the villages and provide access to the local people and resources; however, of late, we have refused to engage in such hospitality because we feel that our relationship with the villagers is very much affected. We can never break the trust of the villagers at the cost of a research project.

Indeed, training on the research process, methodology and data collection practices emphasizes empathy, understanding and compassion to view your research subjects, not as data but as research participants. However, over the years, we have witnessed a lack of genuine compassion for the people whose problems or lifestyles may enlighten the lofty ideals of the research project, but their plight fails to move the researcher to establish an empathetic human connection with the ostensible 'research subjects'.

The fear of speaking out

As described in the previous section and in other chapters, we noticed grave mismanagement by contracting researchers, but we have little formal authority to challenge the people engaged in such practices. Time and again, we have been overworked and underpaid. Even though we have faced grave injustice in the research process, we do not want to raise our voices against the contracting researcher because of the differential power relations. The professor handling the project is the principal investigator and occupies the topmost position in the project. He/she is a superior, all-powerful and well-known person in the academic world. He/she holds command over his/her subjects, has been a guide to several scholars and has produced many literary works. Research scholars generally dream of being associated with him/her. They keep a set of volunteers who help them to hire us to work as facilitating researchers.

How can we point out such a person, who commands so much respect in academia? Particularly those of us who are budding scholars are afraid to speak up, since it will mean our career will end before getting started. If we do so, our future will be highly affected, and maybe we will not get opportunities to be part of projects in future. We at times cope with adverse situations for getting associated with esteemed institutions and working with reputed professors, still hoping it can add to our academic credentials.

We know that we are not in a position to fight against the powerful and influential person, and it seems futile and even counterproductive to raise our grievances in public. One mostly assumes that the researcher's power could shield him/her from any consequence or adverse outcome. We find it a pragmatic approach to sideline/silence ourselves from the project instead of voicing our grievances.

Contracting researchers might feel that we are happy and satisfied with whatever they have offered since we often remain silent, but the reality is that we prefer to remain silent than express our dissatisfaction. The silence which prevails in the academic world against such injustices varies from individual to individual. Some of us have, at times, tried to raise our voice for change, but it rarely leads to any change. Sometimes when we are told that we might not get any credit for our work, we decide to quit the project. However, the contracting researcher then often tries to convince us to come back with new promises. One amongst us talks about her experiences after voicing her grievance:

> *While the project began, I was been [sic] told by the researcher that every penny belongs to the research facilitators. I was quite happy to be a part of the project from prestigious institution. But as all started, I found that I am being fooled and exploited. After spending several months in doing the project and journeying to and fro, I received INR 5000. When I complained he/she did not reply and instead asked me if I want my name to be there in the project. I understand for I have nothing in written, I cannot claim anything. I don't want my name to be left out for I am new, and I also want recognition.*
>
> *The researcher is powerful and can at any time tarnish my image if I go against him/her.*

We are aware of the contextual power play and political games between the researchers; things cannot be categorized into black and white, but instead, there are many shades of any group. Even when someone categorizes a person into a group of oppressors, they have different shades and interactions. Hence, we do not want to defame or shame anyone by publicizing their names. While working as facilitators, things have happened to us repeatedly, but we continue to work because we believe this would bring those social and political issues to the limelight that are close to our hearts. We do not have access to such public platforms where we can shout out to the people. Thus, in a way, we consider this a part of our political activism, community service and social responsibility to work for a project that aims to highlight the topics we are keen to pursue. At times we find topics closer to activism. We feel that, at least through researchers' publications, people will come to know of the Adivasis, their problems and their injustices. Hence, we continue working as facilitating researchers.

Reflections from the eastern DR Congo: Brain thefts through faulty arguments by self-proclaimed protectors

By Oscar Abedi Dunia, Eric Batumike-Banyanga, Stanislas Bisimwa, John Ferekani Lulindi, Bienvenu Mukungilwa, Francine Mudunga, Lievin Mukingi and Darwin Rukanyaga Assumani

This is where we plan these themes. When we have planned, we propose such and such a theme based on such research that we have carried out in such and such area. So, we think that such and such a theme would be important for us to understand such and such another thing. Together we do these analyses. We do even develop the tools here. After we have developed the tools, we collect the data in the field. We return. We discuss these results, how to analyse them and out of these analyses, we sort of validate the results. What is the job if it is not just to go, put small things into it and publish? But why am I, who participated in all these steps, missing in the results? What more do you want me to contribute with?

We agree with our colleagues in India and know very well how our contributions are precious and share the experience of being silenced and non-recognized. So, what is then the process that leads up to this silencing? There is often a close collaboration between facilitating researcher and contracting researcher during the fieldwork, but as in the case of India, we generally do not hear so much from the contracting researcher afterwards. If the fieldwork is conducted together with the contracting researcher, once back in his/home country of residence he/she sometimes contacts us for questions of clarification and understanding. Other than that, there is usually no more contact. When we do the data collection without the contracting researcher, we sometimes put our names in the end of the report that we send to him/her with the idea of appearing in the final paper. But we hardly ever get further than occasionally to the section of acknowledgements. Often, the contracting researcher does not even send a copy of the final paper for which we collected the data and contributed with our knowledge. You could call it brain theft. As one of us concluded during the workshop:

> No one sees us. We are like little robots in the machinery. We produce the results, but no one recognizes our place. We don't even know if we exist. A ghost may be there, but no one sees it. There are people who have the ability of seeing ghosts and saying that they exist, but most people don't. We participate in the research, but we are not visible. The result is always the same: it is the contracting researcher who is identified as an expert on a certain theme in the DR Congo while we are invisible, like eternal ghosts. Nevertheless, we are the ones who worked on the themes and who often have many years of experience on a certain research topic. Thanks to us, the contracting researchers move up the academic ranks, while we, in most cases remain stagnant. One of us has been working as a facilitating researcher for the past twenty years, but his name has never appeared as an author of a research article, and he has not been promoted at all. Another one has, within several research projects, worked on the topic of research ethics, but even in this case, the co-publishing only included the names of the contracting researchers. In addition, nothing improved financially for the facilitating researcher even after these projects on research ethics.

One argument that is sometimes presented to us is the alleged negative aspects of joint publication or production. A research article by multiple people, the contracting researchers tell us, does not have the same strength as when it is attributed to only one person. According to them, it is easier to see the effectiveness of a single person; in the case of a co-publication, the reader would have difficulties judging the different authors' contributions to the paper. But in practice, research projects carried out in conflict zones in DR Congo are always collaborative; a foreign researcher never carries out a research project on his/her own. Claiming this is just a matter of hiding the truth on the ground. In addition, it is not uncommon for contracting researchers to co-publish together.

Sometimes, contracting researchers point out the dangers for us facilitating researchers, as a reason for not stating our names. Of course, armed groups are present in the area, and we ourselves sometimes refuse visibility because of the risks. But currently these kinds of threats are not what they used to be and above all, we believe that we are better placed than foreign researchers to assess the risks and therefore to judge whether we would like to appear as co-authors. Moreover, as we write in Chapter 5, they sometimes put us at risk in publications in other ways, by insisting to disclose the names of respondents and central interlocutors.

The contracting researchers know that the publication of an article will make them visible and possibly lead to their promotion. From our understanding, in the climate of academic competition, seeking to retain the data and publish it under their own names is a way of retaining the power. There are a few experienced facilitating researchers among us who have sometimes had the opportunity to co-publish with a contracting researcher; a visibility that has been of great importance; their experience and expertise on certain themes were recognized and for those affiliated with universities, the publication can give a possibility of reaching another academic level. In addition, publications are tickets to academic conferences or symposiums at international level. But as mentioned, these cases are rare.

Sometimes, we wonder if the non-inclusion of facilitating researchers in the editing of a document and in conferences is based on the fear that people will find out that we are more knowledgeable on the DR Congo than the contracting researchers who present themselves as experts. By appropriating the data, the contracting researcher deny the facilitating researchers, the opportunity to share their knowledge and experience publicly and thereby, also to be approached by others who may have an interest in promoting them. Of course, being cited has no direct economic value, other than the academic promotion for people who are affiliated with universities. But even for others, there is value in being recognized and possibly recommended to other researchers.

We also believe that the contracting researchers should do more to build our capacity so that we can take on a more active role in the writing phase and participate in symposia. Inviting us is a first step of course, but we also deplore that we are not offered small scholarships for training in scientific writing or information on procedures and finally also feedback on the texts that we send, for instance fieldwork reports. Contrary to the Indian case, few of us have acquired university degrees and titles. Even then our status is not considered. Often, it is as if contracting researchers are collaborating with us reluctantly even if we put in all our efforts and sacrifice our lives for their sake. Instead of helping to promote our role in the project, the contracting researchers indirectly block our voice. We have facilitated work that has given contracting researchers international recognition and made it easier for universities to design projects where they have received a lot of money. When we think about this, we feel a certain bitterness knowing that so few of them have had the reflex to quote the contribution of a facilitating researcher, to write a letter of recommendation or to help opening new horizons, for example, to make it easier for a facilitating researcher to pursue higher education with a master's or a PhD in sight. There also exists amongst us, a desolation vis-à-vis the universities with which we collaborate since they have never dreamt of doing us this favour, despite the flagrant inequalities in access to higher education between our countries. We therefore remain under paternalism and colonization as eternal children.

We are both lost and discredited from this silence and lack of control over the data that we collect. A contracting researcher can write that we are going out into the field to collect data for a little report. But he/she can use this same data to produce other texts without mentioning the name of the facilitating researcher. And, as mentioned in the Indian case, we are discredited in cases where negative critique on the text is referred to us, although we have not even been associated with the final product.

When discussing the deeper causes of this invisibility, we as facilitating researchers from the DR Congo concluded that there are two important reasons. Firstly, there is an imbalance between the Global North and South in the academic system itself. This divide exists in research projects as well as in teaching. The funding comes from Europe, and so also the design, the ideas and even the research programmes. In Africa we are just simple underlings. However, not participating in the development and design of the research project should not be synonymous with lacking the right to appear on the list of authors and /or co-authors of the work.

Secondly, it is the same western system that sets the criteria for appearing as an author or co-author. The contracting researcher sometimes presents these criteria to us by saying, 'I would have liked your name to be next to mine, but the scientific criteria do not allow it.' He/She often speaks of the need to participate in a number of phases of a research project: the design and set-up of the research programme, the data collection and finally the analysis and interpretation of the data. But that excludes us in advance since the design and the set-up of the programme are already done in Europe. The contracting researchers approach us when data is to be collected. At the time of analysis, they give us different reasons for not including us. Even if we may have the skills, we are not invited to participate in this kind of work. If in rare cases we are invited, it is important to remember that publications are not remunerated and that the facilitating researcher who is not affiliated with a university constantly runs behind other means of survival when there is no research project.

Sometimes we are given an opportunity to critique and analyse the data that we ourselves have collected. But since we are not involved in the planning of the writing work, this opportunity often happens when we have other work or income-generating activities. We therefore need to know in advance the month when there will be analysis and interpretation work, so that we can prepare for this period. But we do not know the calendar of the contracting researchers and they do not ask for our availability in advance. The contracting researcher may send us a text suddenly telling us that we just have forty-eight hours to read and comment. If we do not have the time to do it within the deadline given to us, the contracting researcher tells us that we are unable to analyse and interpret. Planning without our involvement indicates that we are not seen as collaborators but data providers. So, the only option left for us is to execute the task. It is humiliating.

If western researchers continue to hide the names of facilitating researchers in the final books and papers, they should come and collect data themselves, walk through all the villages and contact the informants and collect the data, without support from any facilitating researcher in the DR Congo. Since they will not do this, we continue to recommend that contracting researchers and the academic institutions to which they belong to recognize our contribution to their work and our involvement at different stages of a research project and consider how they can support our academic careers as well.

Reflections from Sierra Leone: The importance of various forms of recognition and contracting researchers hiding their ignorance through arrogance

By James B. Vincent

When they have gathered knowledge here, they will just go and add theory, and the framework over there. As long as they are here, we help them to analyse, but when they leave, we don't know the actual outcome.

This chapter reflects well our experiences in Sierra Leone. Here, we try to contribute with issues that either strengthen the findings or add dimensions to what our Indian colleagues have mentioned. We notice that even in our country, there are facilitating researchers who are junior staff at the university – however, not amongst us. This is especially common when the contracting researcher or a subcontracting facilitating researcher is a university professor at a local university. Some active university students have also successfully created small research institutes catering for international researchers and NGOs and kicked off entire careers upon what started with aiding a professor. Quite frequently in the early stages, such work is unpaid, at times mimicking teaching assistant structures at the university, but also apprenticeships which is so central to learning a trade in Sierra Leone. Frankly, we come up, expecting many years without proper pay where seniors in our chosen trade make the money, whilst we learn from them, and wait for our turn.

As suggested by the India team, facilitating researchers do not participate in a project for money only. Learning the trade, getting recognition and eventually receiving status are part of the game plan. Therefore, it is not that strange that many of us local research partners 'never negotiate or quibble for money', but if many of us, early in the career accept little or low remuneration, it comes with expectation of fringe benefits, such as informal help with school fees, medical bills, etc. Sierra Leonean contracting researchers understand this but frequently we have ended up at loggerheads with northern contracting researchers who are ignorant of our culture. At times a low salary, or fee for a work, implies from our side, that in the informal contract there is a debt intended to be repaid in the future. Debt is negotiable, but it cannot be unilaterally cancelled.

As discussed in Chapter 5, a fair number of us have also experienced how contracting researchers, at times, fail to deliver to the local community to the extent that we have to use our own money to meet minimum requirements. This may be needed in order to get appropriate security for the team that is visiting, but also in order for us to be able to return with other groups. Yet, still quite frequently, we are accused by local communities of aiding their exploitation.

A point made in this chapter was particular important: that is how researchers who do not understand customs and norms etc., hide their ignorance through arrogance. On the surface it may come out as elitist, snobbish or even racist, but digging deeper we often see that it is a common pattern of insecurity. Yet, still when the contracting researcher starts explaining to local communities what is right or wrong about their behaviour, lectures them and frequently takes a moral high ground, it often results in a less well-intended local community who either resist the study, or who in a semi-polite way fabricate findings.

Just like our colleagues in India, we see the value of official certificates and recognition. Those of us who have been collecting certificates have found it very advantageous. On the other hand, facilitating research in a good way for one contracting researcher often leads to more work. We can easily see how contracting researchers form part of networks wherein recommendations mean a lot. Furthermore, we have our own networks which are also of extreme value. Within these, we also share experiences of how we can do good work, what kind of payment we may ask for and at times who one ought to work for or not. Contracting researchers are not all that good. During our workshop we divided them into three categories: the good, the bad and the ugly.

Just like our Indian colleagues, we seldom see the final projects, we often do not know if we are acknowledged for our part at all, or if the contracting researcher pretends to have done all the work. Rarely do we know if and when the research we have contributed to is published and where. In very few cases we have had the possibility to lay our eyes on it. We do not know if we are in the acknowledgements. An interesting exercise that we discussed during the workshop would be to locate the researchers' publications and see if our names are there.

Our colleagues in India talk about facilitating researchers not being invited to conferences. We agree. Yet if our work is for an NGO/humanitarian agency and being presented in Freetown then some of us have been present, but even that is rare. One of us who has worked at high-level on gender issues has been presenting her research at conferences in West Africa and was invited to a high-level panel in Beijing as well. But even within the gender movement, she has the feeling of being betrayed, as others present her findings as theirs. Twice she has found her work published by others. That has made her leave the gender sector and instead choose social assessments for mining companies as she has better control of her work.

5

Managing various aspects of insecurity

Oscar Abedi Dunia, Elisée Cirhuza, Pascal Kizee Imili, Evariste Mahamba, Jérémie Mapatano and Lebon Mulimbi

I am the one going, the one protecting you. You don't even know the risks I'm running there. You are in your air-conditioned hotel – I am in the field. I collect, I analyse the data. I come and give you the report and there you are happy, and you tell me: you are a good researcher. A good researcher, but then? You don't really pay me for it. This is where sometimes you are not grateful for the effort of the locally based researcher, and this is what hurts. My health, my safety.

The quote above underscores the conclusions drawn by one of us in the workshops in the eastern DR Congo. The theme of this chapter, as stated in the heading, is how we try to manage various forms of insecurities. As this book focuses on insecure settings, the reader probably will assume that the chapter will focus on the insecurity we experience in relation to conducting research in the midst of ongoing armed conflicts. Certainly, we will share our experience of that, and our exposure to a range of risks, such as arrests, beatings and threats. Yet, these kinds of insecurities are not the only ones we experience. We also have insecure livelihoods. In contrast to most contracting researchers most of us do not have a stable income that is sufficient to cover daily expenses. The situation of many of the research subjects is of course even more dire.

In short, our insecurities are not simply about the threats of violence connected to the armed conflicts, but about livelihood and mundane matters such as paying rent, school fees and medical bills, and contributing to food on the table. Without a stable and sufficient income this is not an easy task. This aspect of insecurity that we face will also feature in this chapter, not simply because it reflects our realities, but as it also is deeply related to our exposure to other risks connected to the work we do as facilitating researchers. Our insecure positions in terms of access to resources and livelihoods increase our vulnerabilities to other risks. As we will describe, it reduces our ability to negotiate and forces us to take risks in order to secure an income. Yet the reverse is also true. While conducting facilitating research clearly provides an income, conducting research in risky environments is often very costly, and as we will demonstrate in this chapter, we often have to cover many expenses from our own pockets.

This chapter will proceed as follows. We will first provide an overview of insecurity in terms of livelihoods, including accounting for the various expenses that we need to cater for and often not get compensated as well. Some of these were also mentioned shortly in Chapter 3, but here we discuss it more thoroughly as it is an important aspect of our insecurity and shows how conducting facilitating research not only provides us with resources, but also drains those very resources. After this we will attend to the insecurities and risks we face while conducting research in a setting marked by armed unrest. Here we will also account for how contracting researchers who accompany us to the field sometimes become security risks through inappropriate behaviour.

Our economic/livelihood insecurities and how these reduce our possibility to negotiate

As facilitating researchers, we often have limited possibilities to influence or negotiate wages and working conditions. The contracting researcher is the one who has access to research funding and who sets the aim and scope of the research – including budgets. While we, as described in Chapter 2, sometimes have had inputs for the project in the form of providing new ideas, we are seldom consulted when the research project is put together. The way we get to know about a project is simply when we are contacted and asked about helping out with fieldwork once a project has already received funding. We are rarely consulted when such budgets for field research are put together in applications. Moreover, global budgets or even specific budgets for field research are rarely communicated to us when we are engaged to do research.

In our reflections in Chapters 2 and 6 we have provided some important details in terms of the different positions that some of us at times occupy. To repeat briefly: some of us sometimes are also intermediaries as facilitating researcher who are contracted to engage more facilitating researchers. Yet, even such a position rarely entails accessing information about global budgets of projects. What is provided to people in such positions is often simply a statement of the funds available for fieldwork and the task at hand. However, occupying such a position in a particular project offers some benefits as it sometimes includes additional funding for planning and organizing, sometimes in the form of a few months' regular funding. Moreover the tasks are more often stipulated in written contracts.

Having such a position as an intermediary can offer much more privilege compared to the facilitating researchers who are in turn subcontracted. Whether sub-contracted directly through a contracting researcher from the outside – or via another Congolese facilitating contracting researcher – such work most often takes the form of day labour, where you get paid for the days you spend in the field. The daily fees most often also include reporting of the data that is collected; hence such work is something we are often supposed to do every night when we have finished data collection.

The rates that we get vary. Either we get a salary with additional money for transportation, communication and accommodation, or it is just a fixed lump sum. In the latter cases, the commissioning researcher often simply tells us 'if you want to do the fieldwork, I have USD $40 [per day]'. The sums paid to us vary and we have been paid as much as $20–50 per day, which is quite poor considering the workload and the costs we cover ourselves (see the next section) and the increasing costs of living. Also, for many of us who do not have a regular income it is very difficult to make ends meet, also given that the income is so irregular. Sometimes we are only provided with the possibilities of a few days of fieldwork per month and at other times, months can go without any opportunities at all for some of us.

Moreover, the remuneration is particularly insufficient given the risks we take. When we go into the field we often think 'what if I will die now. What will happen and who will take care of my family. Are the risks I am taking now really worth it?' During the workshop many of us recalled experiences of how we have taken too many risks. One of us recalled how he, after a period of no work and thus being desperate, said yes to a job he shouldn't normally say yes to. He said yes going into a very volatile area where he had never been before, without being able to make any preparations. He had no connections and not even phone numbers of the local chief and only knew his first name. He describes fieldwork as being parachuted into an unknown very dangerous situation. While he, as anticipated, encountered a lot of problems during fieldwork and initially received several threats, he eventually managed to collect the data and come home safe. Many of us have similar experiences of saying yes to work which are simply too risky, in order to bring in money for the family.

It is very difficult for us to refuse, given our living conditions. Most of us care for many family members – including children – and struggle to do so through various forms of temporary work. We often feel that the commissioning researchers take advantage of our precariousness and therefore our inability to refuse what they offer. Given our insecure incomes we often feel obliged to submit to the requirements and conditions of the commissioning researcher, knowing that there is a great competition between facilitating researchers. We fear to be pushed aside. We feel that researchers from the Global North are rarely interested in knowing our difficulties and that they only want our services for which they pay very poorly. There is only one person among us who categorically refuses to go to risk areas, especially if safety is not considered in the contract. For all others, it is difficult to refuse a job opportunity.

Many of us have a feeling of being exploited by the contracting researchers. We feel they often take us for machines and do not respect us or consider our rights and the management of our time. We are often burdened with heavy work involving strict deadlines on working days that must not be exceeded. And if you exceed them, you will do so on your own expense. Not seldom we, looking at the density of the questionnaire and the distances on the field, can calculate that the work may even take fifteen to sixteen days. Yet, the deadline is restricted to ten days only. Hence, our working hours can be from 5 am to 10 pm or even more. This pressure leads some facilitating researchers to take risks to complete on time, such as attending places later during the day than recommended or not following all safety precautions. There is also a risk that the data is not well collected. In addition, the pressure combined with the insecurity sometimes causes us psychological stress.

Most commissioning researchers pay the salary due as agreed, but some of us also have experiences of non-compliance with payment agreements, which is difficult to manage given our lack of financial stability. For instance, for one of us, a daily salary of $25 for three months was initially agreed. However, at the end of the mission, the commissioning researcher only paid for a month and a half saying that she/he did not have enough money in her/his budget. In these kinds of situations of non-respect of conventions (even verbal), we have very limited options. In cases of late or missing payments, we rarely get an apology from the contracting researcher. Often, the researcher simply stops responding to messages. What is worse, some of us have many times reluctantly agreed to work with such unreliable researchers again at a later stage in time, due to our insecure livelihoods – hoping this time around it will be different.

Managing 'additional costs': Healthcare, transport and communication

As accounted for above, the two aspects of insecurity that we experience, that of financial insecurity and insecurity connected to conducting research in a volatile setting, are deeply interrelated. Our insecure position in terms of access to resources and livelihoods increases our vulnerabilities to other risks, as it reduces our ability to negotiate and forces us to take risks in order to secure an income. Yet the reverse is also true. While conducting facilitating research clearly provides an income, conducting research in risky environments is often very costly, and we often have to cover parts of such expenses from our own pockets.

One example of such costs is connected to health and different forms of injuries we get. As mentioned earlier, foreign contracting researchers are covered by insurance when working in conflict zones. But we, the facilitating researchers who do a large part of the fieldwork, are not insured. If anything happens to us, there is no mechanism in place to cover medical costs or compensate the family in the event of death. Psychological stress is not considered at all. As already mentioned, in many cases, we are only granted a lump sum per day in the field and it is difficult to request that benefits, such as insurance, should be included. We have been calling for these aspects to be considered in our contracts for a long time, but so far this has never been the case in our missions for academic researchers from foreign universities.

As concluded in Chapter 2, research conducted for other international organizations is often better in this regard. Most of us also perform facilitation and data collection services for other actors, particularly non-governmental organizations (NGOs) and bilateral or multi-lateral development cooperation actors, such as United Nations (UN) agencies that produce reports and studies on the local situation. While the lack of visibility of our work tends to be the same, these actors are more acknowledging when it comes to the needs of the facilitating researchers who accompany them. With them, we often have higher wages and contracts with insurance that also include the health of our dependants. In addition, they most often provide us with vehicles or motorcycles to go into the field.

While contracting researchers may offer to pay for hospital care if illness or injury occurs during fieldwork, they seldom do so in cases we collect additional data for them after they have left or are engaged to collect data without them altogether – as is often the case. Sometimes they pay part of the costs, while we have to cover the rest ourselves. One of us recalls that he had a motorbike accident on the way to a field site and damaged his leg so badly that it required medical treatment. While the contracting researcher, who by then had left for Europe, paid $100, the facilitating researcher had to add $125 himself from his own pocket for the medical bill. Hence, he had to cover an accident that happened while at work himself, something that the contracting researcher would never have to do, if it happened to him/her. In addition to that, he also lost several months' income as he was immobilized for quite some time.

As we will exemplify here, some of us have also experienced violent attacks in the form of beatings that have caused not only psychological traumas but also physical injuries that required medical treatment. Sometimes, the commissioning researcher covers these expenses, if he/she is willing to. Since it is not stipulated in contracts or in insurances, we are left at the mercy of the contracting researcher in these cases and have no rights. Moreover, while the contracting researcher sometimes covers the immediate medical expenses, some injuries have more long-time effects. One of us is still suffering the consequences of beatings he was exposed to when he was arrested due to a research project he was working on. The loss of income that this implies is of course not covered by insurance.

This brutal difference when it comes to the value of a person's life leads us to question if we are really considered human beings at the same level as these contracting researchers who hire us. We are the field researchers who collect data, analyse and discuss the results. Then, when the contracting researchers publish, they appropriate the data. We cannot comprehend what would justify this great imbalance and segregation. It is inhuman.

Apart from costs attached to illness and injuries, a good number of other situations also generate additional costs, and it is generally the facilitating researcher who must pay these costs out of his/her own pocket. It is often very difficult to get an advance on our salaries and the amount that the commissioning researcher provides us initially to cover transport and accommodation, is often insufficient. We have already touched on the transportation problem briefly. As we have explained, the areas from where data has to be gathered are unpredictable and risky terrains which often generate considerable costs for transport. In remote areas, international researchers go – if they go – by Land Cruisers, or by air, facilitated by UN transportation.

Even if travelling on foot is not authorized for the contracting researcher according to the safety policy of his/her university, he/she does not seem to object to that risk. When we go by ourselves, we often get a limited amount to manage transportation ourselves, frequently through a combination of public transport and motorbikes. Yet, this is often not enough, and sometimes we also have to walk on foot. Different places are not frequented in the same way, a factor that is often not reflected in the amount given for transport. Instead, it is frequently the same sum regardless of the place where we have to go to, and the quality of the roads. Sometimes, we encounter problems when we return after fieldwork if we have had a lot of expenses and fall short of cash. This can be due to the additional costs described in this chapter, new road barriers we have to pass, etc. In such cases we sometimes try to borrow money from others as we are afraid of asking for a salary advance. Because, coming back to our situation, refusing the given conditions may imply that others are ready to accept them.

Often, for communication as well, we end up paying ourselves either in part or completely. As described in Chapter 3, we need to devote a lot of time preparing for fieldwork, to get information about the often rapidly changing security environment in a location, to arrange for meetings and interviews, accommodation, etc. In short, we make many phone calls before and during fieldwork to ensure that data collection is run smoothly. Such communication can add up to substantial costs that we often have to cover ourselves at least partly. The fact that only small parts of that sum is paid in advance often creates problems and not seldom – as with transport – we borrow from others until we get the payment and can pay back.

Managing additional costs: Resolving dangerous situations, creating access and caring for research subjects

Costs can also get added up when we intervene to resolve worrying or even dangerous situations during field trips. Here we would like to share the example of one of us who experienced a serious incident with a group of contracting researchers. The latter risked being killed because they had moved around in a dangerous area where some actors had got the impression that the contracting researchers were meddling in a conflict. When trying to intervene and negotiate, a facilitating researcher himself was quite severely beaten. Also, after the departure of the contracting researchers, the armed actors forced him to return and pay them a large sum in order to 'resolve the matter'. The facilitating researcher still receives threats by telephone. The sum he paid was never returned by the contracting researchers, although it was thanks to this facilitating researcher that they were able to escape – and subsequently also return to do research. Situations like these are hurtful and cause trauma. There is no economic compensation and no support to us despite our dedication to do everything we can to rescue or protect contracting researchers.

Moreover, as mentioned in Chapter 3, without small sums in our pockets to offer key gatekeepers and officials as well as respondents, we simply do not have access to the data. While researchers with long experience know this and often set aside a sum for this, this is not always the case. We then add from our own pockets, afraid that the contracting researcher will think that we cheat them or are bad negotiators.

Obviously, we recognize that there can be problems with giving money to access data and we are aware of the reasons for the reluctance to provide such funds. But we would like to emphasize that we work in conflict zones where armed groups are present. A militia leader who accepts to provide data will ask in the end for the 'chief's drink', 'the chief's cigarette' or the 'chiefs massage'. There are a lot of terms that are used locally: to reciprocate and give something back is the appropriate thing to do according to cultural norms. It is often difficult, even dangerous, to try to resist.

During the workshop we had for this book we discussed 'the NGOization of research', referring to a growing tendency among NGOs to always 'pay' the research subjects to agree to answer questions and provide data. When we do academic research, the same informants naturally expect something from us also. This is a situation that certain researchers and academic institutions in the North appear to have difficulties understanding and discard as totally unacceptable. We would therefore like to clarify a bit from our standpoint: it is not really a question of 'buying information', rather a form of thanking for the availability and for the time. It would be different if the researcher reported before the interview that he/she pays ten dollars for a certain number of interview hours. In this case, we could definitely understand the risk of influencing the data collection. But in rural areas, people go to the fields to work in order to feed themselves and if we take three or four hours of their time for an interview, it seems like quite normal human courtesy to give a small sum or buy drinks at the end of the session. It rather represents a gesture of thanking the person and of ensuring good relations for future research. We must always remember that it is not our right to ask questions to people in any locality. Who are we to come and ask about the armed groups or how the population is experiencing cholera?

We would also like to point out that in the localities where we collect data, the populations live with extremely limited means. So, even before we ask questions, humaneness challenges us. We can come to someone's house for an interview and find his/her wife and children sick. As a member of the same community (although we may not live in the exact same village), we can easily imagine ourselves in that position. So, if we have the possibility, we do act with humanity, even if it digs into our field budget and even if we are instructed not give money to a person that we are going to interview, according to the academic rules. As with small 'thank you-sums', this does not mean that we are paying for the information or that we risk distorting it.

But, of course, with the contracts that offer maybe $20–50 a day, it is hard to deal with these additional charges which are small but multiply when we conduct a lot of interviews.

Managing conflict-related risks

In Chapter 3, we mentioned the insecure environment that we operate in and the considerable risks that come with our work, particularly when the research is sensitive and disturbs the interests of certain authorities. These are soldiers of the regular army, police officers, members of armed groups and agents of the National Intelligence Agency – actors by whom we can be considered as friends or enemies depending on the context and the situation. Asking questions on land management, conflict dynamics and violence, corruption and other sensitive issues comes at enormous risks.

There have been several cases of kidnapping in our areas in the past, for example a well-known situation where two foreign researchers were kidnapped for two days. Since then, there is an increased awareness within foreign universities that our zone is dangerous. As a result, more and more contracting researchers refuse to do fieldwork themselves or are not allowed to. Instead, they send us. We often have the impression that the contracting researchers do not realize the risks for us. Again, the harsh competition between facilitating researchers for the contracts implies that there is no need for the contracting researcher to consider arrangements to ensure our safety. The former agrees to risk his life because he/she is in need and lacks a guaranteed future income. Conducting fieldwork successfully despite the dangers means money – even if it is often meagre – and a possibility of being recommended for other projects.

Many of us have been exposed to grave risks and been threatened during fieldwork. As mentioned already, some of us have also been arrested and beaten. So far, and obviously as we are able to write this, we have been lucky – even if a few of us live with both physical and psychological lasting scars. Most of the times we feel that we have escaped only by the grace of God. One of us recalls one time when it was not possible to go by motorbike, and he had to walk a certain distance with his team to arrive in the setting for conducting interviews. Just shortly after they left the destination, armed men came in and opened fire and a few people were killed. Rumours went around that it was the research team that was the real target of the attack. Up to this day he still does not know if this was the case, and has avoided going back to the area. Situations such as these compel us to focus on the need to consider how one should act if a facilitating researcher is assassinated. Who would take care of his family?

Another field researcher recalls a time when he was collecting data for a contracting researcher and was alone in the field. The location was suddenly attacked by an armed group, and he was caught in the gunfire between the attacking armed group and the one present at the location. Like many other villagers he fled into the forest and walked three days in the bush with only cookies that he had in his pocket to eat, drinking water from streams. After having walked 25 kilometres in the bush, he finally managed to access the road and arrive at a safe location.

Through these situations, we have come to realize that our security depends primarily on ourselves since we have no support from the contracting researchers. We develop our own protocols or security mechanisms through our contacts with local authorities and by creating a climate of trust with the population so that they take on the responsibility for our protection. But often when we enter a very insecure area with a sensitive research topic, we have the impression that we can only rely on God for our security. In cases where we go to the field together with the commissioning researcher, we not only have to worry about our own safety – but also about the responsibility of ensuring the safety of the contracting researcher during fieldwork.

Once the fieldwork is over, the contracting researcher goes back to his/her home country, but we stay put. We are continuously visible in the areas and thus exposed to risks. However, once back in his/her country, the contracting researcher rarely considers the safety of the facilitating researcher he/she collaborated with after the fieldwork. Here too, we would like to recall the role of the facilitating researcher to serve as a bridge between the commissioning researcher and the local population. In Chapter 3, we mentioned how the lack of feedback to communities causes a research fatigue. But even worse, this problem may also create hostile situations the next time we go to the same places. The disappointment of the population on not seeing any change or improvements, or even being informed about the research results, risks igniting feelings and provoking threats to us.

We have already exemplified previously, how threats often come after the contracting researcher has gone and are then left to deal with this ourselves. Often such threats involve efforts to press us for money for the threat/problem to 'go away'. While contracting researchers may offer to resolve such issues if they occur during fieldwork, they seldom do so when such situations occur after fieldwork, and he/she has left – which is most often the case. As concluded, the same applies to costs that may relate to accidents of illness attracted during fieldwork.

Managing the contracting researcher as a risk

In the environment in which we operate, the behaviour of the contracting researchers also represents a considerable risk. Several of us have experienced how questions outside of what had been agreed upon resulted in dangerous situations, even death threats. In these cases, the contracting researcher starts asking questions on topics other than those agreed on or making insensitive comments, for example on customs, religion or armed conflicts. In such situations, not only the commissioning researcher is endangered, but also the facilitating researchers who accompany them. It is therefore a serious problem that can put us at considerable risk.

One of us recalls an instance when he worked with a researcher who initially – when he agreed to work with him/her – explained that the research project was about agriculture and land tenure. Yet, once in the field he/she started to ask totally different questions about armed groups and illegal incomes. The facilitating researcher quickly realized that he/she had not been honest about the real focus which they first discussed, and which he agreed to facilitate. As a result of the sensitive questions, also posed in an impertinent and direct manner, the village chief and population started to accuse them of being spies. While the contracting researcher was at another nearby location, a mob gathered around some of the facilitating researchers. They were handled roughly, and the mob threatened to kill them. The main facilitating researcher was finally able to help free the others but had to stay himself in captivity. Only after giving away his cell phone, he was eventually allowed to leave. When he asked to be compensated for his cell phone, the contracting researcher replied that it was the facilitating researcher's responsibility to come to terms with 'his brothers'.

While asking sensitive questions in an inappropriate manner can constitute a risk, lack of knowledge and respect for local customs and beliefs can also endanger the team. A field researcher recalls how he was acting as a facilitating researcher in a locality where the population was Christian and very religious. The contracting researcher who had engaged him started talking about religion in very disrespectful terms. Several respondents heard the comments and got very upset and contacted the pastor, who in turn ended up calling the police asking them to stop the research mission. The situation became very hostile, and the facilitating researcher received death threats and it was only thanks to his contacts with a soldier that the team managed to escape the location.

Another factor that can put the whole team at risk is failure to follow safety recommendations. For instance, one of us worked with a commissioning researcher whom he tried to convince not to go for interviews in a certain locality because of the ongoing military operations. However, the commissioning researcher maintained his/her decision and told the facilitating researcher that if he did not go, he would no longer be hired, and the commissioning researcher would instead pay other people to accompany him. Out of fear of losing the job that supported his family, the facilitating researcher felt obliged to follow the commissioning researcher's will. Ten minutes after the team arrived in the area, there were bomb detonations and rattling of bullets. Luckily, they were all able to escape without any injuries, but yet again it could have been different. Many other people in the location died that day.

Risky situations also sometimes appear when the contracting researcher does not want to devote enough time to visiting authorities. As explained in Chapter 3, meeting with various local authorities is crucial in order to conduct research in a safe manner. Yet, especially contracting researchers with limited previous experience of the setting, sometimes do not always understand the importance of these visits and appear to see them as unnecessary bureaucratic protocols and a waste of time. Most of us have experienced this, and the consequences that can follow. One of us recalls how he was working with a new and fairly young researcher who was very pressed for time and did not want to spend too much time on official visits. While the facilitating researcher argued that it would also be pertinent – given the topic of the research and the tense situation in the area – to pay a visit to the army commander at the location, the contracting researcher did not see the point in this and refused. As a result of this five soldiers came to the interview location and interrupted the session, demanded papers and started to interrogate not only the researchers, but also the respondents in a very hostile manner. This situation which was traumatic not the least for the respondents could certainly have been avoided if the contracting researcher had only agreed that he meets the army commander first.

A final problem related to the behaviour of the contracting researcher is the publication of sensitive data particularly in texts and reports that are made readily available. As we concluded in our reflections in Chapter 2, we object to the tendency of foreign researchers to decide whether it is too dangerous for us to appear as co-authors. We believe that we are better placed than foreign researchers to assess the risks and therefore to judge whether we would like to appear as co-authors. Moreover, given the limited preoccupation with our safety otherwise (as described above), we often feel that it is just used as a pretext to not invite us to be co-authors. A further indication of the lack of real concern for our safety is a failure to listen when we urge contracting researchers to not directly name interlocutors in reports. Not naming the subjects is of course quite common in academic texts, but in more policy-oriented research, the contracting researchers often want to name the interlocutors, particularly when they are influential people. Often this is done without listening to our worries and really considering the possible risks for the facilitating researcher involved. As many of us have tried to explain, even if our names do not feature in the reports, our identities will be known as people know, that, we worked with the particular contracting researcher and author of the report.

For instance, one of us was threatened by a leader of an armed group for data published on the assassination of another armed leader. When he shared these threats with the contracting researcher, the latter took no precautions. The facilitating researcher was eventually whipped and interned in the hospital and his phone was confiscated. But the commissioning researcher was not willing to help or repair the damage even though the reason for his suffering was the publication of data where the real names of the interlocutors had been mentioned. Up to this date, the facilitating researcher continues to suffer the consequences of these events. Others amongst us have also received threats in person or by telephone after the publication of the real names of certain people who have appeared in sensitive situations, for example as alleged perpetrators of violence.

In this chapter, we have discussed our working situation, how the commissioning researchers, when they pay us, do not take into account the conditions in which we operate, and ultimately also the additional costs that are associated with the field research. The commissioning researchers and their institutions have the main responsibility for this situation; they are the originators of the research projects, and they should treat people they contract in the way they themselves wish to be treated. Above all, they should consider our realities. Of course, we also have a responsibility when we accept deplorable working conditions. But, in this chapter we have elaborated three important reasons which push us to do so: the precariousness of life, the uncertainty of employment and the strong competition between facilitating researchers. During the workshops that took place as part of the research project preceding this book, the value of having a union for facilitating researchers was repeatedly raised. This is a theme that will be further elaborated in Chapter 8.

Reflections from Jharkhand/India: The lack of concern for our safety and being pushed into risky situations

By Anju Oseema Maria Toppo

It is troubling to read the experiences of facilitating researchers from eastern DR Congo, but at the same time, it goads us to introspect on our experiences of serving an integral yet unacknowledged role in the research process. We make a case that our insecurities and vulnerabilities as facilitating researchers are no different from our colleagues from the DR Congo. Given the ongoing exploitation and oppression of the local people in our region, the area has witnessed movements to assert indigenous rights, leading to armed conflicts between the state, the Adivasis and the Naxalite movements. Apart from the emotional investment of the local people, these movements sustain through immense human, economic and logistical support from the local people. The state and its security apparatus are out to reinforce the so-called writ of the state and thus resort to indiscriminate use of force and violence on the local people.

Regrettably, the researchers we work with fail to comprehend such movements' inspirations, objectives and intensity. Moreover, the high-profile researchers are oblivious to the grave risks we face while conducting fieldwork to gather first-hand information, the most critical part of the research project. On several occasions, we have to face the wrath of the local police, including harsh interrogation; the police have searched our bags, checked every page of our diaries and notebooks, scrolled through our phones and have issued open threats to stay away from the affected areas.

The situation for fieldwork is indeed perilous, for we know some of our friends have had traumatic experiences of spending days in the police lockup or even faced imprisonment. We, too, fear for our safety and liberty, given that the local police enjoy unrestricted power and thus we can easily be labelled as militants, insurgents or anti-national, and may end up as convicts with false allegations. We are considered as the bridge between the researchers and the field. However, most of the time, we see ourselves as the disposable link between two different worlds. The researchers imagine that by issuing instructions over the phone or sending us the guidebook for fieldwork, they have equipped us with all the requisite skills and safety measures. For their part, the researchers have ticked the check boxes of providing formal information about fieldwork in conflict-affected areas.

However, ground realities represent an altogether different world from the imagined fieldwork area; at times, we find the situations unimaginable and have to return from the site without access. The researchers sometimes get angry that we have failed in making any headway, not appreciating the danger we face or hostility we encounter. Nevertheless, should we explain our predicament and the imminent threats, even the most sympathetic researchers often still ask us to negotiate our access to the field somehow and try alternative arrangements to collect data. One of us recalls the reaction of a contracting researcher at one of such situations: '*Do not make excuses. Others are able [sic] to report on the situation, so why are you not? You have to get things out.*'

Some of us have taken shelter in the villages during armed conflicts. One of the biggest threats to personal safety is that on most occasions – unless we have very strong local contacts – both sides in this conflict suspect us as impostors masquerading as researchers to gather intelligence for the other side. The local villagers suspect that we are informants of the police, while the police think that we are stirring up violence and instigating the locals. This is a catch-22 situation, and we constantly have to deal with several uncertainties. We are aware that no help would be forthcoming, should we end up in an unfortunate situation, particularly from those who do not respect our labour and hand over a meagre amount for our perilous assignments. Contracting researchers do not have to face the hazardous situations that we have to endure, yet they pay us a tiny proportion of the total funds they receive for the project. We know this, but we agree to do work because we need money; this is an important source of income for many of us, and our families depend on us. However, while working on these research projects, one certain thing is that our safety is the least of the contracting researchers' concerns.

On occasions apart from being the target of local police and armed insurgents, the local goons also target us; sometimes openly confronting us. Given that kidnapping to extract ransom may occur, it is a scary scenario for us. During our stay at the villages, it is not just us but also the people or the families we stay with who become targets for such threats. There are instances when the local villagers who extended hospitality to the visiting contracting researchers faced severe consequences for their so-called insubordination by hosting outsiders without prior approval from local crime gangs, local militant leaders or even local police. There were instances when the host family lost some of their members as revenge killings for allowing outsiders to stay in their homes.

In some cases, we cannot directly approach the people we intend to interview; instead, we rely on local contacts, mostly the agents. For example, if one wants to interview malnourished children or their families, one must first contact the local health worker to reach the target population. However, in most cases, people do not feel free to share their opinions in the presence of the agents. On the other hand, in their absence, we have succeeded in getting various information, showing how the local people have been deprived of several privileges. We record their experiences and hardships and propose certain policy changes to help the local people. However, once the state authorities hear about these recommendations and our interventions, they threaten us, instruct us to not visit the place again and not publish any follow-up report. Threats over the phone are common for most of us. We do not lodge complaints against them, for we know they are influential people and can easily harm us. Therefore, in such situations, we try to keep away from these sites. Contracting researchers have either not faced similar situations or are impervious to our situations, most of the time, and they would reprimand us for our incompetence or worse for dereliction of duty. Somehow, we have concluded that most of these researchers are not just unsympathetic but also supercilious.

Our insecurities have grown with time due to outsiders' exploitation. In Jharkhand, there are very few instances where some of us have not been exploited by the contracting researchers. They often act as if they are trying to promote our careers and serve our best interests, so they would offer us to work in their research projects. However, the reality is rather stark. We know that these eminent researchers have received a large pool of money for the work. However, they would try to pay us the measliest amount. There are times when some of us have not been given a single penny for the extensive and hazardous work. We cannot even ask them to offer better working conditions and proper payments given their positions of power and how much influence they wield institutionally and through their networks. In most cases, these arrangements are verbal, and the lack of any formal, written contract allows the contracting researchers to get away with their unethical work practices. Inadvertently or not, our work for the project goes unpaid, and our contributions to the research output are unacknowledged eventually; as facilitating researchers, one must reconcile with a complete erasure from the project.

Reflections from Sierra Leone: Broken promises of remuneration, the problems of expectations from others and the various risks we took

By James B. Vincent

This chapter resonates well with our experiences. Our role in the research chain is marred with dangers of different kinds. We have navigated our research teams through numerous checkpoints, negotiated and not seldom been forced to set up conspicuous relations with rebel commanders during the war. However, the research scene really exploded directly after the war. Although less dangerous on paper, on the ground many former combatants remained as capricious as they were during the war. As much research focus was on the combatants, for a rather long period after the war, we had to approach our fields with great care in order not to put ourselves, our families and individuals in the local areas at risk. As described by our Congolese colleagues, a great source of stress has also been the responsibility for the contracting researcher, a stranger at times behaving awkwardly like an elephant in the field. Trying to keep everybody safe and satisfied is quite a feat. Several local journalists assisting international journalists were killed when they were on work-related missions during the Sierra Leone war, but as far as we know, no facilitating researcher has been killed or severely injured during, or after the war. But that has probably been more a question of luck than anything else. We know of one who was in a car accident and lost a limb whilst returning from fieldwork.

Just as noted by the DR Congo team, our main insecurity is related to uncertain livelihoods, where field-related problems – for instance a misunderstanding in one area due to a contracting researcher asking the wrong questions – could block field access for an extended period of time. Quite often access implies having to grease some palms and keeping elders, commanders and other elites happy. Activities like these are often done informally and at the time hidden for the contracting researcher. We pay for access with our own money and hope to get reimbursed by the contracting researcher. Only the more experienced contracting researchers have volunteered to reimburse us for these kinds of expenses, and if we suggest that this should be done, both our motives and our honesty are questioned. Quite the contrary, some researchers deny us reimbursement arguing that paying for information is both unethical and may distort findings. The consequence of this is that we either spend too much of our own salary or that local communities deny us access to the field the next time. Failing to pay such informal fees during the war could furthermore have lethal consequences.

As also noted by the DR Congo team, during the war many of us fought hard to survive and even a token given by a contracting researcher would lure some of us into the field. Even if it meant going behind rebel lines. Today we often have some form of contract, but back then many of us just rose to the occasion and left without knowing what mission we would go on and what payment it would yield. We took the risk, hoped that being with a contracting researcher would give some kind of protection and prayed to God that it would clear some kind of economic pathway up ahead. To us it actually worked to our advantage, but many others tried their luck only once, felt used or risked too much and left. We all have had some bad experiences. One of us recalls how he was once promised 300,000 Leones [at the time about $100) for two weeks work. But later the contracting researchers said they had run out of money and did not pay. Another one of us remembered a similar case, and also how he at that time managed the situation:

> *We had some problems due to money business. A team of young researchers did not want to pay us what they promised, but then we reported them to the immigration authorities, and they forced them to pay. These [contracting] researchers were students, and they didn't have proper documents to do research so in the end that forced them to pay in order not to end up in worse problems.*

We are of course very much aware of the differences in salaries between contracting researcher and facilitating researcher. We also understand that costs are much higher in the countries where the contracting researcher lives, and furthermore that they have higher expenditures in Sierra Leone. But we generally feel that differences are huge. We 'feel' because we can seldom be sure. We agree with what our colleagues from the DR Congo have mentioned; that even if at times the contracting researcher can share a ToR or a project proposal, it never includes a budget. During all our facilitating research works none of us have been offered to see a project's full budget. This creates a lot of room for speculation. Are we given tokens only for our work? Are the contracting researchers becoming wealthy because of our work? As one of us concluded:

> So, the way they benefit compare it to me. It is zero! So, what they pay to sleep for one week passes the amount of the whole work I do. And I have no security. And we have signed no contract. The risk we take, compared to what we earn is not enough. We do it because we want to learn and at times, we have no other options.

Oftentimes working with contracting researchers from the Global North raises huge expectations from friends and family. Although our salaries are often quite modest, and we spend some of it during the fieldwork, friends and family think we get rich overnight. When we come home with little or nothing it often create tensions when we cannot pay for house rent, or the school fees for siblings. At times it has driven wedges between us and loved ones. One of us recalled his experience:

> So, after we [a project with UNICEF] did research in my own home village they started to complain. They started accusing me of giving money to other villages. But they [UNICEF] had decided to build wells in other nearby villages not ours and they did not give me much money at all. But it did cut off relations between me and my father's village. Since 2006, I have not gone to the village. I don't know if there would be problems if I go, but I still do not have the [financial] resources to go there. I don't know if they will drive me off or fight me. Maybe they will just look at me in a bad way or ignore me. I can't stand the thought of that!

The above cases relate to another issue brought up by the DR Congo Team: the contracting researcher is at risk during the few weeks or months they are in the field. We remain there. The UNICEF study above shows one long-term outcome of this. But others may be more direct. It is not just the contracting researchers or the facilitating researchers who are at risk. It may even be the family of the facilitating researcher. If we are associated with a researcher who behaves badly, or even later on writes about something sensitive, it may be detrimental to our families.

6

Beyond a narrow North/South divide

Anju Oseema Maria Toppo

We, the facilitating researchers, consider it our privilege and a matter of pride to have the opportunities to contribute to the fruition of the high-profile research projects that we consider significant and relevant to our local communities and their problems. However, the sense of self-exaltation is often short-lived, and in most cases our aspirations of realizing societal and personal goals through our engagements with research projects remain unfulfilled. As described in earlier chapters, receiving the due recognition and appropriate recompense for our labour while working with researchers from foreign countries is rare. Yet, as we will demonstrate in this chapter, it would be wrong to point fingers only at the researchers coming from the Global North. It is imperative that we look beyond a narrow North/South divide and take stock of the domestic scene and the inherent exploitative practices of the research processes based within the country. This chapter aims to look at this facet by accounting for our experiences of exploitation by fellow Indian researchers.

As stated in the Introduction, we in Jharkhand availed of this opportunity to write this chapter since we have the most extensive experience working together with national researchers. This is perhaps due to the comparably strong position of Indian academic institutions and access to research funding. Hence, and in contrast to what appears to be the case in Sierra Leone and DR Congo, Indian academics have more access to research funding from national and international sources. Some of these scholars come to our setting to conduct their research and engage us to facilitate their work.

As already alluded to, we find no significant difference between researchers from abroad and those from India. In fact, on several occasions, our compatriots surpass the foreign visitors in manipulating us to further their own agenda, objectives and ambitions. Multiple instances mark inequalities between us, the facilitating researchers and 'contracting researchers' in the national context. We are familiar with the exploitative research behaviour prevalent among more privileged Indian researchers. They tend to occupy high-profile positions with esteemed establishments such as state or central universities, plum research institutions and influential administrative roles within the government; they wield considerable power and authority and acquire copious adulation from society. More than the quality of the research output or the ethical integrity of the research process, their earlier affiliations, networks and access to privileged information about the system empower them to appropriate most of the research initiatives from the domestic and foreign agencies/institutions.

Setting the stage for our exploitation as Adivasis and women in a national context

Given our experiences with foreign and national researchers, many of the themes addressed here are similar to those described in previous chapters. This also raises the question as to why there are so many similarities. The exploitation we face with foreign researchers is often explained in terms of colonial history, racism, and continued and substantial power inequalities between academia in the Global North and South. So why, then, are we equally exploited by our own compatriots? Part of the explanation lies in the unequal structure of academia itself and the power differential it inheres, leading to the exploitation of younger, more junior scholars, which can be observed in most academic settings – discussed in greater detail in Chapter 8.

The exploitation we face is also connected to our status as Adivasis and women, so we would first like to explain our setting in details. As we explained, the 'we' here consists of a diverse group. However, most, like myself, are women and are also particularly involved in research on women's rights and empowerment and gender equality in Jharkhand, as mentioned in Chapter 4.

The Indian social structure is hierarchical along intersections of caste and class. Historically, the Adivasis have stayed outside the mainstream caste and class hierarchies, having less access to positions of power and resources. The contracting researchers are mainly from privileged backgrounds. They consider Adivasis as mere data providers and not as knowledge producers. They consider Adivasis far less educated and knowledgeable about transforming the data into knowledge materials. This bias against Adivasis is reflected in denying due recognition of their academic labour and intellectual contribution and refusing to make appropriate payments. They refuse to believe that they would not have been able to produce any output without the involvement of the Adivasis. Many amongst us feel that the contracting researchers have preconceived notions or outright prejudice against the Adivasis, especially women. In most cases, the Adivasis are caught unawares (although not ignorant), so the contracting researchers present themselves as knowledge producers. This is evident in their references to Adivasis as 'backward', 'unintellectual' or people without a sense of history.

Our accounts of the experiences here also reflect the fact that most of us are women. National contracting researchers have particular prejudices against Adivasi women. These researchers are often quick to pontificate on women's issues, gender rights and equality among different sexes. However, the behaviour of many of these mostly national women research associates towards us belies any commitment to those lofty ideals. Some, for instance, insist that those amongst us who are married should ask their husbands to support us with the fieldwork, bear all the expenses, arrange logistical supplies and do the household chores to set us free to do scholarly work. Contrary to the public posturing, these same ideals of gender equality do not hold any validity in their own life. Ironically, while most of them work on projects focusing on women's empowerment, they, as we will demonstrate in this chapter, find all the different excuses to delay or deny payment when it comes to paying the women involved in the fieldwork.

Expressing dismay with the research process, one of the facilitating researchers said:

I think we should try to get our own projects. Now we have enough idea of how work has to be carried on. At least we will have money to offer to the ones who will be acting as facilitators, not like the ones for whom we are working. I was not even asked of my expenditures. I was just handed over Rs. 5000 only for visiting the field which is around 250 kms from Ranchi. The researcher knew it well that my husband stays in the said place. So neither before, nor after was I asked of my expenses. I was supposed to stay there for more than twenty days. The archive was located faraway from my residence. Sometimes my husband used to drop me but most of the times I had to arrange my own transport. Literally my husband had to bear all the expenses. Even for the xerox that I got it done from the archives. I know I cannot spill this in front of the researcher for one is a known figure and my career will be at stake.

Side-lined also in supposedly inclusive research projects

Those of us who are part of academia have understood that national contracting researchers prefer to work on research projects with foreign funding from renowned institutions. The national researchers focus on high-profile projects from prestigious institutions because these assignments allow them to participate in policymaking circles and help them in their career progression. It would seem a natural choice given the eminence, the public profile and the availability of a large pool of funds involved in these projects against the domestic or in-house ones. However, this preference does not mean that the national researchers disassociate themselves from the in-house projects; they tend to manage several different projects by assigning most of the deliverables and tasks to the research associates or facilitating researchers like us.

As mentioned in Chapter 4, we have noticed a new trend in projects to hire people from diverse backgrounds to implement diversity and inclusivity in hiring research staff. This is often the case in research involving national contracting researchers engaging us. Yet, similar to contracting researchers from Europe or the United States, much of this new trend of hiring people from diverse backgrounds looks good only on paper. People like us get very little information and are relegated to work as field workers with practically no input into the conduct of the research process. One of us had the following experience while working on a research project:

> *I got to work on a project to study young people's preferences towards politics and their understanding of social standing. One of my acquaintances shared the details of this project with me; a university professor who led this project used to hire research assistants and young researchers for this assignment. Most of these research assistants were paid for the project. I contacted this professor to work on the project since its focus area was closely aligned with my own field of study, and I was keen to gain some valuable experience. The professor informed all of us, the research facilitators, that it was a collaborative project and that a prestigious institution in Singapore funded it. The funds were allocated accordingly, and we were promised experience certificates from other reputed professors supposedly associated with this project. I was involved in the fieldwork, fed in data, and regularly also used to formulate a preliminary report of the completed work. I received remuneration, but the arrangement was different from what was promised at the beginning of the project and before disbursements, we had to sign the receipt that we had received the amount. Moreover, I never received any experience certificate for my work on the project. I never got to see the final report for which I had put in efforts to collect the data and prepare preliminary reports. Forget about recognition; I am not able to access what I contributed.*

Many of us have had similar experiences of national researchers engaging in certain unethical practices to realize their ambitions, even in these supposedly more collaborative projects. In this project, as in many others, once a certain number of research personnel are in place, a core committee is formed by selecting some facilitating researchers. This core committee then makes most of the operational and logistical decisions about the conduct of the research and organizes, plans and allocates the areas (of research) and the corresponding team members for field visits. The entire process of constituting the core committee appears democratic, equitable and impartial, given that the core committee comprises facilitating researchers.

However, fundamentally this core committee is anything but impartial and equitable, and the Adivasis are never selected to be a part of this select group of researchers. The prevalent culture of privilege and patronage in academia allows only select upper-class and caste members among the facilitating researchers to join the core committee. Though there is slight or, at times, no difference in the payment but the members of the core committee have the privilege to choose nearby locations, as non-core committee members, we cannot make such decisions and are generally pushed to work in distant places. It is a fact that working in towns and urban areas is much easier than getting into some unknown far-flung villages. Thus, exploitation begins right at the start of the research process; for us, the Adivasi-facilitating researchers, we are never seen as equals; the decision-making rests in the hands of a select band of mostly non-Adivasi individuals.

We never get to know details about the funding institution; at best, we are told that the project is sponsored/funded by a prestigious institution abroad. The India-based researchers of these foreign-funded projects often depict a promising picture of shared and collaborative work culture and intellectually enriching and financially rewarding work experience that would potentially launch our careers as authentic researchers in the field of study. However, accurate information about the institutional affiliations, management structures, leadership roles, work practices, emoluments and other rewards is never provided in detail.

On most occasions, we only interact with the core committee; we rarely directly interact with the lead researchers based in India. We undertake field visits, gather primary data and prepare fieldwork-based preliminary; in all cases, we submit the reports to the core committee, which then forwards these reports to the researchers. As already mentioned, we hardly get to hold personal conversations with the researchers; there is no formal agreement between us, the facilitating researchers and the contracting researchers. We have nothing to show to claim anything, for we are not handed a formal written document; instead, it is always a verbal commitment. Many of us who have worked as facilitating researchers have no certificates, not even hand-written letters by the contracting researcher, because everything is done verbally. We understand that contracting researchers receive huge sums for working on foreign projects. However, as will be further elaborated below, we hardly receive even the minimum wages for the kind of work we do.

Some of us feel that overseas contracting researchers have at least some ethics and accountability, but national contracting researchers can often be corrupt and selfish. They look at this association only in instrumentalist terms, where the facilitating researchers are seen as necessary but dispensable. It is not surprising that the national researchers belong to this country where research ethics are neither adequately valued nor firmly administered. The national researchers are keen to establish a hierarchy in the research project, arrogating themselves and relegating facilitating researchers to superior and inferior positions. We realize that our contribution to the project is vital. However, for these researchers, the trials and tribulations we undertake for the data collection are transactions that can be compensated with some petty amount. Yet, as we describe below, such remuneration is sometimes lacking.

There is a popular yet misplaced notion that an Indian researcher would have a greater appreciation of junior scholars and up-and-coming researchers' difficulties than someone from abroad. In the case of contracting researchers from India, they either appear indifferent or oblivious to the ground realities and precarity of the young researchers. When we try to raise specific issues and seek their help in resolving potentially dangerous situations, we do not get any sympathetic response from the other end.

Many reputed university professors are part of several research projects; since most of us are pursuing PhDs under their supervision, it renders us vulnerable to exploitation. The senior academics would involve us in their projects without our consent and randomly assign fieldwork as part of our research. Our work for the project is always compulsorily voluntary, unpaid and unacknowledged; however, we cannot refuse this forced labour, given the power equation between the PhD candidates and their supervisors. We are obliged to visit remote villages, make valuable contacts, prepare a questionnaire, interview people, gather official records and sometimes travel interstate to collect data from archives. Moreover, we are supposed to prepare all the reports, edit, proofread the preliminary reports and prepare the final reports. The senior academics want us to travel to the field during the day and visit them in the evening to share our findings and experiences. None of us can recall the senior Indian academics having accompanied us to the field; instead, they sit in their comfortable places and prepare the final reports based on our fieldwork. This ongoing process does not stop with one project; most of us end up working on two or three research projects, and juggling all these responsibilities without any reward is daunting. Apart from all these, we live in a constant fear that any mistake or oversight may sour our relationship with the contracting researcher, and in such a situation, there is no recourse but to abandon any plans for pursuing a PhD and give up on an academic career.

Poor and unpaid remuneration

As mentioned initially, it appears that contracting national researchers who visit Jharkhand from other Indian states imagine the local research facilitator as someone untrained, unemployed, uncouth from a backward state. A local person is seen as someone who is hard-pressed for money to survive and will gladly accept even the smallest remuneration. On most occasions, these interstate researchers would stay in the state capital or other major urban centres, expecting us, the facilitating researcher, to venture to the remotest areas of Jharkhand. There are often no provisions for our travel, lodging, food and other logistical necessities; if we try to negotiate, they ask us to maintain a record of working hours, travels, hotel bills, etc. and submit it to them. However, once these bills and proof of expenses are submitted to them, inevitably, we often do not receive any money for these expenses. Most of us have faced such situations wherein the researcher refuses to pay for food and lodging, should we stay with our acquaintances, claiming such a stay was free of cost. Though in real life, we do not visit unannounced at our acquaintances' or friends' house and when we do so we share expenses; as women, we take precautionary measures to ensure our safety.

Senior national contracting researchers often portray a glowing picture of the potential opportunities and accrued benefits once the funds are released. As young researchers looking to establish our credentials in the field, we work enthusiastically without thinking about written contracts or proper negotiations. At the same time, we are also concerned about public image and do not want to appear selfish or greedy, asking for potential opportunities and financial benefits. We agree to search the archives and libraries, toil for days and weeks, do fieldwork and compile the reports. We make arrangements and pay from our pockets to meet the expenses.

However, once we hand over the data and other material to the project team, even though the official funds have been released, most contracting researchers do not provide us with our financial entitlements. Some researchers keep the money to themselves, while others may return some portion of the allocated funds and trumpet their ethical behaviour and honesty. One of us shares the following experience with an esteemed professor from a reputed institution:

> *I was looking for a supervisor to start my PhD, and I approached a professor from a prestigious institution in Ranchi. The professor told me that by the time I prepare my synopsis (detailed research proposal), I could work as a research assistant with him on a project. Initially,*

the professor clarified that I would not be paid for my work as a research assistant. However, a few days later, the professor assured me that a request had been made to the director to offer me the post of a research assistant. I was told that formal employment would offer me a reasonable amount as a one-time payment. I was quite happy with this assurance since I was new, and this seemed like a big opportunity. I joined the project to gain knowledge and experience and improve my research skills; however, I received no emoluments whatsoever for all the work I put in for the research project. The professor made me work on the research project on an assurance that was never followed up.

We sometimes need to interact with government officials and local authorities to access official records. These officials often ask for bribes to access the records; if we report these demands to our national project team, they often refuse to engage with any bribe as an unethical practice. Nevertheless, they are asking us to collect data from official records, and they know how the system works. Yet, when we tell them of the amounts requested to access the data, they often blame us for inefficacy or lack of intelligence for not knowing how to negotiate with the bureaucrats. In some cases, the project researchers laugh at our incompetence and assert that we lack communication skills to convince the local officials.

On several occasions, when we have complained about the working conditions and the lack of formal and written terms and conditions, we are sure to lose any chance of receiving our experience certificates. Although we may have provided all the project deliverables with utmost care and diligence, the project team will refuse to provide us with any credential of affiliation on the pretext of unspecified mistakes in our work. The national researchers who hire us to work on the projects seem to consider it a personal favour of allowing us to gain experience and visibility through these projects, and therefore, we should work free of cost. These researchers fail to realize that instead of providing us with visibility, we are the ones who bring them visibility in the field, and we are the critical link between the project team and the people in the field. It is not that the national researchers are unaware of the ground realities, challenges, impediments and risks that we face while working in the field; however, they assign us the most arduous tasks and present them as an excellent opportunity for us to learn and gain experience.

Most of us have also suffered due to bureaucratic failures and a lack of proper record maintenance in the release and allocation of funds, particularly with state projects. The contracting researcher often uses this lack of transparency as an excuse not to pay us adequately, timely and courteously. Many of us work in the universities on a temporary or permanent basis and also as facilitating researchers. Once we become a part of an academic institution, the rules, regulations and procedures do not remain hidden from us. We know the total outlay for the particular project and can estimate the schedule of fund release and its proportionate distribution on other overheads. Occasionally, contracting researchers are bound by time commitments, and they want to start the project from their own savings before the release of official funds. In such cases, the contracting researchers negotiate with us to start the work and wait for the payments once the funds are released. In equal measures, these negotiations are achieved through the power differential between us, the junior scholars and the senior academics, mostly a mixture of promises and threats.

It is noteworthy to mention our belief here that domestic contracting researchers are much craftier than foreign researchers. They are rigid about making any payment and often try to minimize even the most essential expenses; we end up paying for such petty expenses from our pockets. It is quite disheartening to ask for money and support for conducting the fieldwork repeatedly; we usually give up and manage the expenses on our own.

Lack of concern for our security

Most of us have faced hazardous situations and have been forced to leave our hotel rooms at night, make alternative arrangements or take a dangerous overnight trip back to our homes. There are a few non-Adivasi settlements where people do not like the interaction between boys and girls, for they consider it inappropriate behaviour that may affect their culture. On many occasions, we are assigned to work with teams comprising both male and female researchers; the locals find this strange and sometimes react very aggressively towards the team. It has happened to some of us, and we were asked to vacate the rooms at night. The contracting researchers turn a blind eye to these hazards and imagine that the paltry emoluments are fair compensation for all our sufferings. We consider such behaviour of national contracting researchers not just unfair but inhumane. In addition, the limited time and budgets drive us to be in firefighting mode constantly. Most of the time, even we, the putative locals, are not well-versed with all the regional dialects and have to rely on local resource persons for translations. Unfortunately, we run at a loss, for we are not paid for hiring translators; however, the local translator would not engage with us the next time should we fail to offer adequate compensation for their time and efforts.

We are not ashamed to state that some of us have also faced sexual harassment from contracting researchers. Most of us studying in universities have to face awkward situations, and we are not in a position to fight back or bring the culprit to face the consequences. As junior scholars at the bottom of the pyramid of academia, we need to gather knowledge, experience and skills to acquire competencies and collect the work experience certificate to fulfil the bureaucratic requirements. The supervising researchers are aware of this situation and try to exploit our vulnerabilities; several of us have had very unpleasant experiences, such as using explicit language, vile jokes, late-night calls and offensive text messages. Most of us ignore these advances; few of us have made formal complaints but to no avail, since these influential researchers control the entire project team.

Most of us have faced similar situations, and we are sharing one such experience here.

You won't believe if I reveal the name of the person. Even if I expose him, I know I will get into trouble. The best thing I did and I do even today is ignore such people. Can you do me a favour? Through this, can you put this up that details about age and gender should not be asked by the contracting researchers. I think I was kept as a facilitating researcher for I was a fresher and was young. You can understand what I mean. Pay me nothing and take undue advantage. I was doing my work of data collection very seriously. It was almost ten to twelve days working as a facilitator. One day the contracting researcher texted me at midnight and asked me about the problem I was encountering and if I needed any suggestions. I felt good that he was being supportive. The next day he texted me not to worry about the deadlines and feel free to call him up. The very next text stated how he can shape my career. There are few things which I cannot even mention. He stooped so low. This was my first project and I did not have any idea of dealing with these matters. The best and the right thing to do I felt at that moment was to submit and leave. And I did so.

Even less engagement with communities and mismanagement of data

In Chapter 4, we accounted for our experiences of foreign visiting researchers lacking genuine compassion for the hardship of the Adivasis. This is equally – or even more true – for national contracting researchers. We have realized that national researchers lack the curiosity to engage with the people on the ground and are even reluctant to visit the field compared to foreign researchers. Most of them prefer to stay in urban centres and instruct us to work in the field, asking us to stick to the schedule and budget through telephonic conversations.

Hence, it is quite rare for national contracting researchers to stay in the field; however, should they choose to do so, we take it as a personal responsibility to look after them and take them around. Most of the time, their friendliness is 'a charm offensive', and we tend to share our local knowledge, findings and writings on various subjects without realizing their motives. Invariably, these national visiting researchers promise to publish our written pieces in respected publications and academic journals. However, our work finds publication avenues only after our names have been erased from the authorship. The lack of academic integrity is one thing, but this amounts to outright intellectual theft. All of us believe that at least the foreign scholars do not stoop to these levels and publish our written pieces in their names, or even if they have done, none of us has come across such pieces.

We, the facilitating researchers, have been used by these visiting high-profile researchers as tools and instruments to access the field, reach people, gather data and provide cheap or free labour. We hold no value to the contracting researchers beyond the immediate and instrumentalist utility. They do not allow us to act independently, but instead force their ideas, perspectives and even prejudices on us. It is no wonder our thought processes are muddled, for we cannot bridge the gap between theoretical perspectives and prevalent practices. Despite providing good quality, accurate data, the researchers are free to indulge in data manipulation and interpretation, which they do according to their convenience and agenda, thereby either unknowingly misinterpreting or wilfully misrepresenting the views of the people.

There have been numerous instances when we, as field researchers, have meticulously gathered a large volume of data and have reported multiple cases of malnutrition, poverty, public health issues, social deprivations, moral degradation, gender-based violence and caste discrimination. However, in the final reports, the data interpretation is changed to project a very different picture than the stark ground realities. We are highly disappointed to find that data has been completely altered, and the contracting researcher has just mentioned the positive aspects, showing developmental activities, glorifying the state and pointing at the rich culture, language and religion. A complete opposite interpretation is also peddled when the researchers portray the rich traditions, cultural heritage, timeless legacies and local customs as backward. Incorrect interpretation or wilful misrepresentation of data is relatively common; however, should anyone challenge the high-profile researchers, they simply shift the onus of data collection on us, claiming that we did not follow the due procedure or do our due diligence. One of us shared the following experience,

While working on a project I realized that the other part of the story remains unexposed. Misinterpretations are very common or one can say people come up with what they want to show. Most of the researchers have biased opinions about the Adivasis. I once had the opportunity to visit a village and report on malnutrition. I found out that the cows were in plenty but villagers never milked the cow to feed themselves. The reason behind this was that they felt that this was for the calf and nobody should deprive the child of the mother's milk. The researcher had joined us on fields for a day but to my surprise he reported that the Adivasis are very backward, cruel, shrewd. They deprive their children of the available food. They don't let their children drink milk.

Our relationships with women from the villages suffer because of unpaid labour; the women working in the fields take time off their work to spend time with us to share their experiences. However, once they realize that there is no payment for their time, they blame us for wasting their time, so we either pay them from our pockets or damage our relationship with them. The contracting researchers focus on publishing the research findings in their own names and gaining recognition for highlighting the problems. Their scholarly dissertation or policy prognosis may bring them laurels, yet such research outputs fail to make genuine changes or bring relief to women.

National researchers of eminence and reputation can always rely on us, the local facilitating researchers, to act as a conduit, a bridge, a path to approach the inaccessible. However, the unequal relationship is a structural issue with the research process, and there is no easy resolution to these embedded problems. Simply changing the agents will not change the structure. To overhaul the prevalent structure, there is a need to recalibrate the mode of exchange between the contracting researchers and the knowledge producers on the ground. This would benefit Adivasi women whose lives have been a primary research subject.

Their interactions with men and their social positioning have always aroused great curiosity among researchers. However, unfortunately, the ones who are the owners of this knowledge are non-recognized.

Reflections from the eastern DR Congo: Quite different experiences, although we recognize the problems of the house colonizers

By Oscar Abedi Dunia, Elisée Cirhuza, Pascal Kizee Imili, Evariste Kambale, Jérémie Mapatano, Lebon Mulimbi

There is also the house colonizer at the southern level who needs a change of mentality to understand that if I benefit from advantages in my relation to a foreign contracting researcher, I also need to share it with and defend those who do not have it.

Our experiences working with national contracting researchers are quite different from those of our colleagues in Jharkhand. In contrast to the Indian case, Congolese researchers at large have no access to research funding, and the type of prestigious academic institutions and scholars mentioned by them do not exist in the same way in DR Congo. Many renowned and prestigious Congolese scholars attract research funding, but most reside in Europe or the United States and are not engaged in research on the eastern DR Congo. In our case, it is rare to work with national contracting researchers from other parts of the country like Kinshasa or Lubumbashi. Most of the national contracting researchers we work with come from our area, and they occupy that role in between that has been described in Chapters 3 and 5. Moreover, and given that situation, the problems raised in relation to prejudices against certain groups, like the Adivasis in India, do not apply in the same way in our context. While we come from different groups, and ethnic prejudice certainly exists and is a problem in DR Congo, it is not a major issue in our work. The negative experiences that some of us have in relation to national researchers' instead mainly connect to prejudice and a sense of superiority due to education, positions and other privileges.

Yet, as we can see from the Indian experience, the relationship between contracting researchers and facilitating researchers is always defined by an imbalance of power. This imbalance is the crux of the problem and can also be encountered in the relations between Congolese contracting researchers and facilitating researchers. A foreign researcher commissions the academic projects we are engaged in because the local universities do not have the funds to conduct their own research. Often these foreign researchers (generally from Europe or the United States) prefer to set up contracts with local networks of researchers since some perceive it as risky to work with an individual facilitating researcher they do not know.

What we call networks of researchers include research companies, universities or sometimes NGOs. The advantage for the facilitating researchers involved in these networks is the facilitation of contact with other contracting researchers, which offers a little more financial stability: at least we know that we can get assignments with them from time to time – even though it should be said that we can spend up to one year between the assignments. Yet, if an opportunity arises and your experiences fit, you know that you are one of those who will be contacted. Sometimes, network involvement also opens opportunities to participate in trainings or conferences.

However, there are also negative experiences related to these networks. Several of us who have since long been part of these networks can feel trapped as if we are the private property of the Congolese researchers who head these networks. Moreover, there is no long-term engagement, only for a certain research project duration, and many of us are connected to several networks. As mentioned above, work opportunities are often rare, even within the networks, and one can spend up to one year between assignments. Yet, we are often expected to be always available or at least inform the network if we do work for others. If we are on the move, we can be told, for example, 'How can you be in Kampala? Who told you to be there?'

Sometimes promised jobs, for some reason, also do not materialize. For instance, one can get a WhatsApp (social media) message saying that we must do fieldwork a particular week. But when the week arrives, there is no research. One or two weeks pass by, and during this time, the facilitating researcher starts looking for other assignments because he/she does not know if this research work will materialize. Furthermore, while he is on another assignment, he gets the work order for the network. It becomes difficult to handle. By belonging to a network, we must always be available and attentive to the needs of the main researcher of the network. We are really like assistants who sometimes even must carry their bags.

There are also conflicts and power relations in the network where everyone wants to always be on top, the one who gives the orders. There is a kind of competition between the facilitating researchers engaged in the network and efforts to impose restrictions on others regarding what topics they can work on. For example, certain topics are said to belong to certain people, so a person may not be able to deal with a topic in their local zone because there is already someone working on this topic in the network. There are also favouritisms in the network in relation to affinities and affiliations.

Another negative aspect is the impossibility of negotiating the contract in the network. The head of the network has already negotiated with the contracting researcher from abroad without asking the opinion of the committed facilitating researchers. When he accepts certain conditions, he does so on behalf of everyone. We are only supposed to perform our work in the field. Also, it can be assumed that the money left to pay the facilitating researchers reduces with each intermediate level because there are administrative costs.

If a facilitating researcher is hired by a contracting researcher individually (outside the networks), they still have some leeway. Even if, as we saw in the previous chapter, he/she feels pressured by the precariousness of life and the need to have an income, the facilitating researcher still has, at least in theory, the possibility to refuse work for a certain amount and/or he/she could try to impose acceptable working conditions. On the other hand, in the network, ten days equals ten days, even if the research topic is complicated and the question guide is very long. We can be told that 'the deadline is Saturday, anyone who does not present their report in the evening will not have the rest of their per diem at the office'. Also, it is not always apparent that the conditions agreed upon between the network and its facilitating researchers are respected. Often, it is concluded that the payment must be made in two instalments: the first before going to the field and the second after submission of the report. However, it happens that the facilitating researchers submit their reports on time, but the second instalment payment occurs three months after the report's submission. In our discussions within the workshops of this project, we concluded that for our salaries, the possibility of having a written contract and the working conditions is more or less the same whether we work within a network or not. As facilitating researchers in the networks, we remain calm and do not talk much about the situations we encounter in the field. If we express ourselves, tomorrow, we may no longer be employed as facilitating researchers.

Reflections from Sierra Leone: National contracting researchers as outsiders, often lacking the curiosity to engage with the people on the ground

James B Vincent

Research funding for Sierra Leone-based researchers is often hard to get by, similarly to what our colleagues from the DRC described above. Either they are part of a project headed by an international researcher or do commission work inside the UN/World bank or INGO research projects. Many Sierra Leonean scholars left the country during the war and found their way to northern universities. Others managed to get scholarships and received PhDs during the war years. They have been a successful group; many maintain close bonds, do joint publications and get project funding. Only a few of them have returned to Sierra

Leone after the war, and most of those based at the Sierra Leonean universities and colleges are outside the research project funding loops. No research council exists, and other research allocations from within the ministry of education, or other government agencies, are lacking, but at times there are openings for commissioned work. This makes up for a different playing field than the scenario in India. However, we also find several similarities.

The India team states in this chapter that many national researchers lack the curiosity to engage with the people on the ground. We have noticed a similar pattern. Commonplace, they are less interested in going into the field, often appear less prepared and often take for granted that they understand the context. Previously in this book, we noted that this happens with contracting researchers from the North, but here we would like to reiterate that it is even more prevalent with national researchers. Sierra Leonean researchers, in our experience, do understand the ins and outs of our culture better, but 'culture' is not the same across the country, and they often fail to see this lacuna.

Two of us stated the following:

Local researchers do not know anything. Imagine if you are born in Sierra Leone and do not know. They do not know the areas. Often, they solely depend on us.

From my perspective, a local researcher who has not been to a particular area is equal to an international researcher. If you are from Freetown and have never been to Kailahun?

Things often get worse as many come with an air of superiority; they want to show their privilege when they reach the field, and we have experienced that it is often hard to change their preconceived ideas and attitudes. Thus an active learning experience is often hindered. As noted before, this point goes for quite some researchers from the North as well. However, just as in the Indian case, they often see us as untrained and easily fooled by their perceived superiority. They are also frequently less guided by strict research ethics. Viewing their global position as exploited in the postcolonial reality, but thus often fail to see, or at least turn a blind eye to, how they exploit yet others. Sierra Leonean professors have to a lesser extent exploited us than the Indian example gives at hand. The reasons for that may be that only a few lead research projects and that only a few of us are pursuing degrees at the university. However, whilst doing field research with a national contracting researcher, we often have the experience of being at the bottom of the research pyramid. We find senior national researchers complaining about their junior position in relation to even very young, at times pre-PhD level, scholars from the North. However, they pay little attention to how they are treating us.

National or subregional (West African) researchers may be less honest when presenting research findings at conferences or in publishing. Whilst northern contracting researchers seldom share final versions, or may not sufficiently acknowledge our roles, we have experiences of national researchers virtually stealing our knowledge. One of the most senior facilitating researchers, who also works as a gender advisor and consultant for many agencies, gave examples of her research findings being used by national contracting researchers during conferences in both the sub-region and a high-level international conference in China as well as another piece she wrote being published under the name of a contracting researcher. She only found out several years later.

Another issue worth mentioning is that we commonly know our country's language, culture and traditions. It is indeed a key asset. However, we want to reiterate how important it is for a facilitating researcher to know the right language or the traditions of the particular area of the country where research is to be conducted. It is culturally an advantage to being a Sierra Leonean, but many facilitating researchers are born and raised in the capital. They, too, may not know the local language, and although they understand the ins and outs of our culture better, they often fail to see this lacuna. A local researcher who has not been to a particular area is, in many ways, equal to an international researcher. If you are from Freetown and have never been to Kailahun, there may not be that much of a difference compared to a researcher from abroad. Thus, from our experience, having a facilitator who works in the area's language is an invaluable asset. However, to a surprising extent, the contracting researcher pays less attention to this fact.

7

Beyond the bleak picture

James B. M. Vincent, Paul Amara, Peter Bangura, Lansana Juana, Ahmadu V. Kanneh, Saidu Yusuf Kamara and Alie Sesay

In the previous chapters of this book, we have retold our experiences of exclusion and silencing and poor working conditions, including remuneration. Yet, there are always two sides to every coin. Though we have highlighted the bad and ugly sides of research relationships in the previous chapters, most of us have also had some positive experiences, which should be shared for a more balanced, unbiased analysis. During the Sierra Leone workshop, we kept coming back to the mantra: the good, the bad and the ugly. In this chapter, we talk about the 'good', but remember, this is our bottom line:

> *The knowledge they come and take is not cheap. Locals wonder we they come and take local knowledge. They don't pay tax for it. They often fail to go through the right channels. They have the wrong documents. So [people in the] community, country, feel exploited. It is the country who do the losses. We don't gain. The researchers take the money back. We can pay 300.000 Le for one year's house rent. The researcher can spend it for one night on a hotel room. And the food and everything. At the end of the day we don't benefit. So if we talk about percentage it is zero for me! So the way you benefit compared to me? It is zero! So what you pay to sleep for one week passes the amount of the whole work I do. And I have no insurance, no security. So in fact you can just push me away. You don't know my family, we have signed no contract, and if you know where I come from, you will be afraid to go there, because they may arrest you.*
>
> (Sierra Leone facilitating researcher)

The bottom line is clear: extreme inequalities regarding access to resources exist even in positive experiences of relationships with contracting researchers. However, the facilitating research that we have conducted and the relationships we have developed with contracting researchers have enabled most of us to improve simultaneously not only our economic standards, but educational standards and research skills as well. During our workshop we did far from only complain about contracting researchers, we praised them as well. Praise should be given where it is due. In the following section we will go through some of the statements given during the two-day workshop. Learning to know the country and its peoples was one issue brought up:

Together with the [contracting] researchers we come across new things, meet new people. With the researchers we bump into communities we would never do otherwise.

(Workshop participant)

For me. I was born in this country. But I didn't know it [the country], until I worked with X (professor in anthropology). X made me understand this country in a very close way. Especially on the historical side. We went around the entire country, excluding Bonthe Island.

(Another workshop participant)

One of the younger of us highlighted the mutual learning process of research work in a good way, yet perhaps with a hint of irony regarding 'high knowledge':

Working with you gives us a sense of pride. Your higher knowledge. Most of us had just finished secondary school. Academically you learn from us, but we learn from you too.

Many of us were about leaving secondary school and was looking for sponsors to further our education. As previously mentioned at that particular point hooking up with contracting researchers enabled many of us to get into college and in some cases much further. Others had different trajectories but were equally helped beyond the pay check. Two of us received help while setting up websites. One of us stated: 'X created a website for me so other researchers can see my work and link up with me.' For others it implied far ranging changes, but not without challenges. This statement from one of us who was a rebel soldier during the war perhaps highlights this best:

> *I was more or less adopted by researcher X. His friend, researcher Y lived nearby and at times I would help him too. When he left in 1996, I had his phone number. But when the AFRC came to power, I went back to fighting, and I was selling looted goods when I reconnected with Y. So when he came back after the war, I became his research assistant. I shouldn't lie, but all I could think of was that one day I would go overseas. When he wanted to leave, I held him at ransom when I realized he would not bring me along! Despite the trouble I gave him, he has later on connected me to more than ten researchers. Some year later researcher Z left me with a whole Keke [Auto rickshaw]. But I am supposed to pay back small-small. So the researchers have been able to guide me. They reintegrated me. I am really grateful and happy for what they have done for me.*

Most of us did not take active part in the war, but we still found ourselves part of the war economy as another one of us states when commenting on his trajectory as a facilitating researcher:

> *I had a warm heart [acted aggressively] at school, but I was lucky. God is there. During the war I worked selling looted diesel on the black market, but [contracting researcher] X came and put trust in me. Life changed gradually.*

Our positive experiences made it incumbent for us to continue this line of work and prevented us from branching out into other, if not more lucrative, at least more predictable trades. A few of us progressed into proper research and have gradually become competitors in bidding competitions with contracting researchers, we previously worked with. A few of us have also developed long-term friendships with these contracting researchers. Yet, it is important to underscore that such positive experiences are quite unevenly distributed amongst us, something we will come back to at the end of the chapter. We start the chapter by accounting for the experience that is most appreciated, but quite rare, amongst us: that of building long-term friendships.

More lasting friendships

A few of us have had the opportunity of linking and working closely and for a long time with contracting researchers, which has grown to become lifetime relationships. Two of us have developed especially strong relationships. We are on a casual basis in touch with specific contracting researchers and whenever they visit, they stay with us. These extensive relationships started back in the war years. As we elaborate later, it seems that the joint hardships and dangers we experienced during the war years allowed for and facilitated stronger relations that lasted longer.

One of us, we call him Joe, developed such a relationship with a UK professor, whom we refer to as Bill. Bill, who in turn was introduced to Joe by another professor of anthropology (who had earlier worked with Joe), came to do an anthropological study in 2007. Bill and Joe worked together for about two years. During this time, they managed to build a relationship based on mutual trust, confidence and more family-like feelings. Bill, after a couple of years, worked so closely with Joe that he would send Joe to the field ahead of his visit to do research scoping and to 'soften the ground'. Eventually, Bill simply followed the feedback of Joe in most matters. Wherever Joe advised him not to go, he would not go. Bill continues to have a very close camaraderie-type of relationship with Joe to the extent that anytime Joe has a problem, be it psychological, emotional, educational, financial and otherwise, he will always call Bill to confide in him and they will mutually solve it. However, the opposite is also true. Sometimes Bill, when he has no funding available, will only need to ask Joe to do some scoping on a particular theme and specific area(s) and Joe will find ways and means to pre-finance the exercises and be reimbursed by Bill. Until now, the relationship between Bill and Joe is so congenial that the mutual trust has now exceeded working relationship and they discuss virtually on a monthly basis on the phone, even if Bill does not have any work to do in Sierra Leone.

As reflected in this story, these types of friendships are also possible outcomes of research relations. A small number of us had this experience of more long-term relationships resembling family networks rather than working relationships. Often such relations involve an interest and engagement also with our families in various ways, and the contracting researchers become part of the family. For instance, one of us talked about a contracting researcher, he first came to know a long time ago and who at an early stage paid school fees for one of his children. He is now considered like an extended uncle. One of us also had a contracting researcher as the Godfather at his marriage. Such alliances can turn lifelong and extend from generation to generation and from family member to family member as experienced by the anthropologist Michael Jackson and his facilitating researcher-turned friend and the intimate intertwining of two families.[1] Yet, such experiences of very close friendly relations are rare amongst us. However, and as we will account for below, some of us have positive experiences of contracting researchers engaged in advancing our careers as well.

Contracting researchers trying to advance our careers

As concluded in the previous chapters, it appears that most contracting researchers are simply interested in furthering their own careers – often at the expense of ours (not allowing us as co-authors, etc.) Yet, quite a few show concern for, and interest in, furthering our careers as well.

One way of doing this is to facilitate access to educational institutions, pay tuition fees and facilitate scholarship processes in

---

[1] Jackson 2004.

Sierra Leone or overseas. Most of us have received some aid towards furthering our education at learning institutions in Sierra Leone, and two of us have received degrees from European universities through the assistance of contracting researchers, we have worked with. One, we call him Tom, came to work with a professor of governance from a renowned British university; we here call him Clark. Clark came to work on a long-term project on democratic governance in Sierra Leone. The relationship between Clark and Tom started with an introduction from another contracting researcher who had previously worked with the Tom – yet again; a relation was established through work networks and recommendations. Clark and Tom worked together for only one month in Sierra Leone. Yet, Clark expressed that Tom had great capacity and spoke to Tom about a possibility of him furthering his educational pursuit at his institute in the UK. Upon discussions, Clark sent Tom's academic credentials to his department for the possibility of gaining admission into his department. Tom got accepted and completed his studies successfully. After some time, Clark managed to get a partial scholarship for Tom so that he could continue with an MA degree. Tom, who unsuccessfully had been scouting around for a scholarship to do his master's degree for several years, took good care of this rare opportunity to further his education. This opportunity changed Tom's career substantially. He is now one of the few who has gradually become a competitor in bidding competitions for consultancy work with contracting researchers we previously worked with.

Moreover, some contracting researchers have also contributed to advancing our careers in other ways, by providing support of other kind. In Chapter 2, we told the story of a facilitating researcher, which we now name Jack, who started working as a facilitator when he was in Senior Secondary School and was approached by a female contracting researcher, we now name Lucy. As accounted for in that story, Lucy (in contrast to many others – see Chapter 4) kept her promises. She came back to Sierra Leone after the initial fieldwork to conduct research but also helped setting up an NGO focusing on education, which also financed Jack's school fees. Lucy later came to support Jack's future education in other ways, by providing support to start a small business selling mobile top-up cards. It was with this money that Jack eventually managed to get a *Higher National Diploma* (HND) in accounting and finance. There are other similar examples where contracting researchers contributed to enhancing facilitating researchers' possibilities by contributing with means for school fees or side business, or rents or hospital bills in times of crises.

Another way in which contracting researchers can advance our careers – already alluded to in several of the examples provided – is to recommend you to other contracting researchers. As reflected in most of the stories, we have been able to be continuously engaged by recommendations from previous contracting researchers we worked with. Some of us are still recommended to new researchers by old contracting researchers who worked here a long time ago and have now moved to other research areas. This has enabled us to accumulate experiences and knowledge that we can use also in relation to non-academic studies and other similar work.

Lastly, while very rare, it should be mentioned that a few of us also had the opportunity of working with groups of researchers, or individuals who made sure that our names were included in the final reports. Such co-authorships came out of longer and extended collaborations. A few of our colleagues have had such collaborations in Sierra Leone and these have yielded positive dividends.

Enhancing status and opening doors to other opportunities

Our working with academic researchers also opened the door for other opportunities, not the least for working as consultants for major international organizations. We have previously mentioned that a problem with facilitating research work is that families, friends and home communities expect that we bring home enormous wealth. As elaborated in our reflections in Chapter 5, we have all experienced the pressures that come with that.

But there are other positive aspects we ought to highlight as well. One thing that most agree upon is that we felt elated in the eyes of others after having worked with researchers especially from Europe and the Americas. Some of us expressed that we experienced being transformed from ordinary citizens to strategic stakeholders overnight because of our contacts with contracting researchers. This was especially the case if the contracting researchers came from UK or United States as these are two countries, people in the local communities have heard and know much about. Sometimes well-known men and women in our communities saw us as competitors, but in part they also acknowledged that we bring in new possibilities and knowledge. Such knowledge and our links with contracting researchers from the Global North tend to make local strongmen tread more carefully around us. This change in status can also open many doors and provide access to a whole range of other opportunities – besides consultancy work for international organizations – such as business arrangements, positions in civil service or in local politics. One of us rose to prominence as a result of the access he gained with government ministers and even some members of the fighting forces gained through facilitating research. This exposed him to several 'hard to meet/contact politicians' and that even facilitated his consideration for a government position in recent times. One of us also had several contacts and contracts because of his access to 'people that matter in society' through his work with reputable consultants from the North and multi- and bilateral donors.

However, we want to underscore that our experiences differed a bit here. How much your status and possibilities enhance also depends on who you are from the beginning, your social and educational background, and how good you are managing your new status. A few of us feel that facilitating work has only meant very limited changes in social status and opportunities. Here it is important to point out that if a facilitating researcher at the onset of the career fails to bring back resources back to the community, or fails to show any kind of advancement, he/she may instead be considered a failure and the connections with the contracting researcher may be a source of ridicule. You may hear something like: 'Look at you, you risked your life for the white man and came back empty-handed, what a fool you are.' Here, it is worth remembering that there is still a sound scepticism against Europeans and others due to the Atlantic slave trade and later on experiences of colonialism.

Remote research as a reflection of trust and an opportunity for facilitating researchers

In the Introduction chapter, we mentioned the increase of 'remote research practices', that it has become more common to see contracting researchers remain in the comfort of their country or stay in comfortable hotels in safe urban settings, while we the facilitating researchers collect data for them. As concluded in that chapter, this process appears mainly connected to an increasing securitization of academic research where research institutions in Europe and United States have come to regulate and restrict fieldwork access due to security concerns of their own staff.

Yet, the context of Sierra Leone, which provides a longer time perspective, before such increasing concern and regulation for contracting researchers' safety set in, also offer an additional, and more positive, perspective; that such practices also can be seen as a reflection of increasing trust and recognition. In short, we have experienced the increase of 'remote research practices' long time back as well, and even if this certainly is a reflection of several things, we experience it is also a reflection of increasing recognition and trust and of relationships grown to mutual dependencies.

We have experiences of contracting researchers from Europe and the Americas, building relationships to the point of being totally dependent on us for their success. They would never hesitate the slightest on the quality data we will deliver. This can indicate that if the contracting researchers treat the facilitating researchers fairly, mutual dependencies and career opportunities will arise. At times, relationships even early on developed to the extent that the contracting researcher can now stay in his/her comfort zone and confidently ask us to carry out a survey in the field on their behalf.

Earlier in this book, we have been critical to sending facilitating researchers into areas where the contracting researchers can or dare not to go, but in this chapter, we also want to highlight the amount of trust a facilitating researcher must have in order to rely on this kind of data. This trust is often built over extended periods of time and collaboration. Moreover, these collaborations also provide us with additional room for more influence and power over research projects.

We presented a case in Chapter 2 where the contracting researchers could contact the facilitating researcher on phone from his home country and they jointly discussed the data needed for a specific project. At times, the facilitating researcher would even start the study ahead of the arrival of the contracting researchers. A few times, the full field study was carried out without the presence of the contracting researchers. Such arrangements can be really good when resting on mutual trust. It is a model to build upon for remote research. On the other hand, we fear that studies where contracting researchers and facilitating researcher hardly would meet up in real life may suffer from the lack of such trust. Another real problem with remote research is that a contracting researcher who hardly touches the ground in our country will find it difficult to understand the social context the research is carried out in. We have, in earlier chapters, discussed the problems of contracting researchers lacking contextual knowledge and we fear that this will increase with more remote research.

Yet still, as stated in the introduction, the increasing outsourcing or 'long-distance approaches' are not necessarily negative. Instead, they can be seen as a reflection of increasing trust and also offer more power to facilitating researchers and new opportunities.

So why the difference?

In the section above, we have accounted for positive experiences, primarily how our work with contracting researchers has also led to various opportunities, of higher education, enlarged networks and more work. We even provided examples of relations that have grown into long close friendships. Yet, as we have tried to continuously highlight, such positive experiences are unevenly distributed and far from all of us have experiences of researchers who do not simply seem preoccupied with their own careers and wellbeing.

So how may we understand these differences in experiences? In Chapter 8, and as also highlighted by the Congolese colleagues in Chapter 4, the negative treatment, the way in which we are excluded and silenced and made to work under unacceptable conditions are a reflection of the imbalance between the Global North and South in terms of funding of projects, given the contracting researchers in the North hold the power to set the principles and rules of engagement. It is this imbalance which allows contracting researchers to mislead us and sometimes treat us in disrespectful ways.

Yet, it has to be acknowledged that there are differences between contracting researchers. As we somehow jokingly concluded in the workshops, there exists 'the good, the bad and the ugly'. Hence, there are differences between contracting researchers and our experiences differ from one individual contracting researcher to another. Contracting researchers, just like all other people, certainly differ in their personal traits. Some are concerned about advancing their own careers above all, also at our expense. Others are also concerned about us and the research subjects and are receptive, collaborative and interested in our wellbeing.

Yet, beyond this, there are also some other factors which play a role in creating the more positive experiences accounted for. One is the time spent on conducting research. Not surprisingly, if you spend a long time in a context and come back time and again, relations are built and strengthened. That is perhaps why some of us appear to have particularly good relations with anthropologists, as they have tendency to spend more time in Sierra Leone. During this time, they learn to understand our society and behave in respectful ways towards us and the research subjects. Yet, more time in the field is obviously no guarantee for a better treatment of facilitating researchers. Most of us also agreed that contracting researchers who have conducted research for a long time in the country are sometimes the worst and at times limit our opportunities to get better conditions. There is this general feeling that old contracting researchers sometimes seem to want to dictate or rather virtually coerce you to accept conditions when agreeing to work for a new contracting researcher. They tell new in-coming contracting researchers that this is what is possible on the ground and that they should or must not allow the facilitating researcher to demand more remuneration or better conditions beyond a certain threshold. On the other hand, there are also some contracting researchers old in the game who have assisted us to negotiate salaries with new-coming contracting researchers.

One thing though that we identified during the workshop that appears to account for some differences in the relationships we have with contracting researchers is joint experiences of danger and high risk. Such experiences form bonds that are hard to break and trust that go beyond the average. It comes without saying that fieldwork during the war years were times of high risk, where both contracting researchers and facilitating researchers worked under severe constraints. It was basically jungle law/survival of the fittest, and combatants knew as well that the government, or the peacekeepers for that matter, rarely had the power to act in large parts of the country. For the most seasoned facilitating researchers, it was a time of pivotal significance as the most intense and deep-ranging relationships were built during this time with both contracting researchers and local communities. We also expect this set of contracting researchers to inform us about any contacts they want to make with other facilitating researchers, or even institutions in some cases. We expect them to go through us, and further, we expect them to direct new contracting researchers coming to Sierra Leone to us, building our clientele base.

We have over the years gone out of the way to help contracting researchers, conducting high-quality research. As many came into the work during our civil war, or in its direct aftermath, it has at times been done at great risk. Many contracting researchers have taken advantage of our fragile situations, but we must also show our appreciation to those who have walked the extra mile and assisted us when needed. In this chapter, we have discussed how they have aided many of us to further our education; a few even getting university degrees abroad. We have also focused on how they have helped us to establish ourselves as semi-professional facilitating researchers, or entered new career paths, and also the meaning of long-term friendships, built on mutual trust and respect. However, we have so far only in brief mentioned the immediate, on the ground, help we have quite frequently received. Whilst in Sierra Leone many of our favourite contracting researchers have helped us pay medical bills or bought medicine when we have been ill. At times even when our kids were sick. Or our mothers for that matter. They have tossed in money when we have been lacking the means to pay school fees for our kids, or the rent, or even contributed with a bag of rice when we have had a hard time to make ends meet. Some have even helped us by buying building materials and constructed everything from 'Pan bodies' to regular houses. We are self-made, but 'man live by man' (we are mutually dependent), as a popular adage in Sierra Leone goes. This was highlighted in our discussions during the workshop. One of us stated this by saying 'Researcher X opened road [created opportunities] for me' and another one said 'I never thought that the little connection I got back then [when still in school] could lead to all this!', but the positive outburst by a third of us stating: 'I am a success story. My success is on them!', probably drives the point through most clearly. Indeed, we have met the bad and the ugly, but also the good, something that we wanted to pinpoint in this chapter.

Reflections from eastern DR Congo: Much recognition, but 'the good' is indeed unequally distributed

By Oscar Abedi Dunia, Eric Batumike-Banyanga, Stanislas Bisimwa, John Ferekani Lulindi, Bienvenu Mukungilwa, Francine Mudunga, Lievin Mukingi and Darwin Rukanyaga Assumani

I will assure you that it is good work that connects researchers at different levels. Once you have assisted research and you are in salons with other researchers, you have connections with others. But also, it is a job that facilitates or helps you to have a global idea of your own area. It is a work that capacitates.

During our exchanges, the negative experiences of the contracting researchers predominated. However, similar to our colleagues in Sierra Leone, we also discussed the positive sides, in particular, how we gain in terms of connections and the ability to analyse our own area through a research perspective. The facilitating researcher quoted above expressed that even though he was sidelined for publications, he gained other perspectives with which to analyze his own zone and interactions with people in other areas. Also, contact with contracting researchers involves work and therefore income opportunities, although, as mentioned in previous chapters, this payment rarely matches the risks and the workload.

One of us in the larger group also has a very positive experience with an exchange created by a university for which he previously facilitated research projects. As a result of facilitating research work he engaged in, he was provided the possibility to be part of an exchange programme which gave him the opportunity to meet and exchange experiences with other African researchers during conferences in different African countries. These meetings are something we genuinely see as important, as it opens up the world for us and gives us lasting contacts.

However, it is obvious that if there are advantages for Congolese facilitating researchers collaborating with the foreign contracting researchers, it is mainly the 'network leaders' who benefit from them. By network leaders, we mean Congolese researchers who manage the facilitation of a research project for a foreign university and who in turn contract other facilitating researchers locally (in our commentary in Chapter 6, we explain about how these networks work). It is the network leader who is in contact with the foreign contracting researchers and who enjoys possible benefits such as participation in conferences, contact with other researchers and training. One of us who is a network leader was also able to co-publish with a foreign contracting researcher.

For those who are not network leaders, capacity building in the form of small grants and trainings could play an important role in our motivation, self-confidence and ability to contribute. It is necessary that we are sufficiently equipped to contribute to texts and conferences.

Even if we do experience it, these types of lasting close friendships appear to be less common amongst us compared to our colleagues in Sierra Leone. Yet similar to our colleagues, we would like to highlight the differences among contracting researchers and how they behave both in relation to us and the communities. Some are indeed much more respectful, willing to learn and also develop an understanding of the difficulties we encounter, including coming to our aid in times of crises, like sickness or death in our families. However, this is also something that is mostly experienced by network leaders.

Reflections from Jharkhand, India: All is not bleak

Anju Oseema Maria Toppo

I often recall my journey as a research facilitator and feel happy to share my best memories. I have met a few wonderful people who have become family and friends. The relationship between us has grown so strong that I know I have got their back. There is one with whom I have not had any conversation in the past months, but I am sure if I get into any trouble, she would be the first one to ring me up. One of them has gifted me a handycam for my fieldwork. This has been of great use to me as I can record the truth.

Very few of us have had similar experiences as shared by the rest. So far, besides the negative side of research practices, we have also pointed out that not every contracting researcher is insensitive. Few researchers have been kind, compassionate to their research subjects and genuine in their research work. Some of the contracting researchers have closely witnessed our struggles, appreciated our work and helped us in multiple ways. Most of us remember the name of at least that one person, who has kept his/her word, maintained contact with us and has reached out to us in times of difficulties.

Research occurs during a limited period, but few of us have earned some long-lasting friendships within this short span. The researchers have offered great opportunities to three of us; it allowed us to find appropriate avenues for higher education in premier institutions. Through their help and guidance, we have sought admissions and availed funds for our fees and accommodation. In the words of one of them,

> *I never thought of moving out of the city any day for educational purposes but thanks to the contracting researcher who made me believe in my potential and helped me all through. He also shared some of his known contacts with me to make me comfortable in an unknown place. I have learnt so much in the previous years that now I plan of moving abroad for higher studies.*

It is not common, but some of the contracting researchers have had a great positive impact on the lives of few facilitating researchers. Three of us had the opportunity of visiting foreign land either for educational purposes or as speakers in conferences. The contracting researchers have borne our airfare and even our stay.

Participating as speakers in international conferences has provided us with excellent opportunities to share our knowledge with a broader community. As activists working for socio-political goals, we always wanted to present the ground realities to everyone to create awareness and forge associations to seek support and guidance for our initiatives. Finding an international platform to address our issues is undoubtedly a milestone for us as individual researchers and the broader community that we seek to represent. We have noticed a drastic change in the behaviour of the government and the authorities after such events; even the erstwhile indifferent bureaucrats seem too eager to engage with us and give us appointments to meet them in person and to discuss our grievances.

Encouragement and acknowledgement have earned us a name in the academic world. Given an opportunity by the contracting researchers, we have never failed to attend seminars, webinars or writing for a journal or co-authoring pieces. Some of us feel privileged to be placed as co-authors. Many Adivasis fought against the system, but how many people know of them or their struggle? Today, we get the opportunity to reach out to larger groups through contracting researchers. As one of us pointed out,

> *Interaction with contracting researcher has helped me grow confidently. It is not only they who come to know of us, but we also get to know of their society and culture. I have noticed that even villagers pay me more respect as they find me walking with a gora (a local term used for a white man). They feel that I do something big.*

Most of us agree that working with contracting researchers coming from abroad has helped us improve our research skills. We have learnt a lot even by observing them, their body language and the ease of doing their work. Most of us have not had any contact with them after completing the research work, but during their stay, some of them have been very cooperative. We get to know about the world outside, and the challenges and opportunities that exist.

Some of us are happy that even today, some of the contracting researchers call us to know our perspective on a particular issue. Though working with some of them did not benefit us monetarily, they offered us institutional, logistical and scholastic help. Some of them enquire about our future ventures and suggest different means of pursuing these goals. 'Remote research practices' are prevalent in India too, where the researchers depend on us. Some of us are satisfied that the contracting researcher made no changes in the data provided to him/her by us. Their dependencies or trust in us have made us believe in our talents and enhance our research skills. All of us have experienced the good, the bad and the ugly, but one must highlight considerate, generous and benign people in the academic world. It is infrequent to build such positive and enduring relationships, but some of us have certainly formed wonderful and benevolent associations with our contracting researchers.

8

The need of change: What, how and who?

Oscar Abedi Dunia, Maria Eriksson Baaz, Anju Oseema Maria Toppo, Swati Parashar, Mats Utas and James B. M. Vincent

We start this chapter by shortly summarizing the book, highlighting particularly the aspects that are crucial for this chapter, which aims to propose avenues for change. After the summary, we provide a brief analysis of how the silencing and mistreatment of facilitating researchers described in this book may be understood. Such an analysis is crucial in order to set the stage for the following and concluding part which proposes some remedies and identifies actors needed to bring change.

Brief summary of the book

The book has (or at least the ambition has been to) highlighted the diversity among facilitating researchers in terms of our/their backgrounds both when we/they first embarked on facilitating research and present situations (something particularly evident among the Sierra Leone authors). Facilitating researchers constitute highly varied groups both when it comes to educational backgrounds, class, socio-geographical backgrounds, present and past other occupations, and whether we/they engage in research on a more temporary or regular basis. Moreover, we have emphasized that the motivations for engaging in facilitating research differ. While some engage primarily with a hope that this will provide a venue into further studies and academic careers, others (like we have seen particularly in the Jharkhand case) engage as they are committed to making the situation of people in their settings known and visible. Yet others view it mainly as a livelihood strategy. As such, and as we will return to below, the importance put on co-authorship also varies amongst us/them. Yet, as we have demonstrated, facilitating researchers rarely make it further than the acknowledgement section. Moreover, while a wish to become co-authors varies between us/them, all evidently want and have the right to, recognition of the work we/they do. Proper and fair remuneration constitutes one of those ways through which work can be recognized, as in other sectors in society at large, including the academic settings in which contracting researchers work.

That current working conditions and remuneration in most cases are unfair and unacceptable is something that we believe most readers of previous chapters would not object to – particularly given the multiple and crucial tasks performed (see also Bisimwa 2019; Cirhuza 2019). As highlighted in the book, facilitating researchers often perform a range of tasks additional to data collection and translation, such as preparing for the arrival of contracting researchers (if they are to accompany fieldwork); adapting and translating methodological tools; providing access to the field by arranging meetings with stakeholders and acquiring formal permissions; identifying informants; managing expectations of research subjects (see also Cirhuza and Kadetwa Kayanga 2020; Mapatano 2019); making and managing itineraries under tight schedules; reporting data, interpretation and initial analysis of data; and – not the least – managing expectations and risks after fieldwork, when research projects have ended.

Moreover, current working conditions and remuneration are unfair and unacceptable given the risks that facilitating researchers are exposed to and the crucial role we/they perform in ensuring security. The notions of researcher (read: contracting researcher) responsibility and even the idea of 'mutual responsibility' (see introduction chapter) appear not only unfair but also slightly preposterous given the realities in the field. As shown, it is almost always the facilitating researchers who take responsibility for and ensure safety in the field – and even at times have to manage security risks caused by out-of-place and suspect behaviours of contracting researchers.

In a similar manner, the current and increasing concern with contracting researcher safety (see Chapter 1) also appears, not only unjust, but slightly absurd, given the inequality in the risks that contracting and facilitating researchers are exposed to and the highly unequal access to resources available to handle risks. Moreover, and as emphasized in the preceding chapters, facilitating researchers are also the ones who need to handle risks in the aftermath of data collection. As we have demonstrated, many have paid a high price and have been subjected to threats, arrests and physical violence, some that produced lasting physical and psychological scars (see also Thamani Mwaka 2019). In addition, facilitating researchers are often forced to deal with security threats and injuries by paying money from our/their own pockets – thus reducing the often already meagre income gained, further (see also Chiruza 2020).

Answering the possible objection of 'so, why do we/they agree to such work then?' is hopefully superfluous for a reader of the previous chapters: in contrast to most contracting researchers, most facilitating researchers do not have a stable income that is sufficient to cover daily expenses. This not only reduces our/their ability to negotiate and forces facilitating researchers to take risks we/they do not really want to take, in order to secure an income.

Importantly, we have also mentioned how many also engage in research like tasks for other actors, such UN missions and various humanitarian actors. As concluded by most, working with such actors often implies better and clearer working conditions, with contracts and better remuneration, covering also at times, some kind of at least minimum insurance. Hence, it appears that academic institutions – that seem to work in a much more unregulated and ad-hoc way – may have something to learn from such actors.

Broken promises in relation to a range of aspects have been a recurrent theme in the book: broken promises of feedback and continued communication when contracting researchers disappear without a trace after fieldwork; broken promises of remuneration, of career opportunities and co-authorship, but also related to an apparent lack of compassion and respect for research subjects. Yet, we have also highlighted more positive experiences of facilitating researchers and the need to think beyond a narrow South/North divide, as exploitative research behaviour is prevalent amongst more privileged researchers in and of the Global South.

Let us now briefly engage in a brief analysis of how the silencing and mistreatment of facilitating researchers described in this book may be understood, based on existing literature and also some interviews conducted with contracting researchers within the bigger research project, which the project forms part of. As part of the wider project, Eriksson Baaz, Parashar and Utas also sought to get a further understanding by talking to contracting researchers working in insecure zones. These conversations were aimed at specifically understanding their (contracting researchers') views about the ongoing ethical issues in the field and the state of the art. The conversations were conducted both through individual interviews and through presenting the project in various academic forums. More research is clearly needed in order to assess the relative importance of different explanatory factors. Yet, a preliminary analysis is crucial in order to set the stage for the following and concluding part which proposes some remedies and identifies actors needed to bring change.

How should we understand the state of the art?

The lingering after-effects of colonial pasts

The problems of exploitative relations between facilitating researchers and contracting researchers described in this book must clearly be understood as a result of a number of intersecting factors. One of those which we clearly cannot escape is colonial history. As Sanjek (1993) showed, the systematic silencing of facilitating researchers forms part of colonial history and the 'intellectual colonialism in the study of "other cultures"' (1993: 13). Since colonial times, people and societies in the Global South have been studied and dissected by scholars from the North. Right from the beginning, such a study/research has been made possible through individuals in the literature mainly – if named at all – called research assistants. Again, as Sanjek (1993) concludes, since the very beginnings such professional researchers and 'ethnographers – usually white, mostly male – have normally assumed full authorship for their ethnographic products' and 'the remarkable contribution of these assistants – mainly persons of colour – has not been enough appreciated or understood' (1993). In short, the ways in which the unequal relations accounted for in this book, forms part of patterns developed during colonial times, and is difficult to deny even for the sternest critic of post-colonial studies. Academia and research clearly constitute one of the areas visibly displaying 'how decolonized situations are marked by the trace of the imperial pasts they try to disavow' (Gikandi 1996: 15).

Such traces are discernible in North-South knowledge production, beyond the issue of the silencing and exclusion of facilitating researchers. They are clearly visible in the global economy of knowledge production on the Global South which is still dominated by white scholars from the Global North, who continue to claim to be the experts on societies and conditions in the Global South (see also Buhendwa Nshobole 2020; Cirhuza 2020). The power in the global economy of knowledge production on the Global South is still located in and held by academic institutions and publishers in the Global North. While the bulk of research now is conducted by researchers in the Global South, such research still struggles to be acknowledged by prestigious publishing houses and journals in the Global North. As concluded by Collyer (2018: 69), knowledge produced in the Global South continues to 'be systematically marginalised, dismissed, under-valued, or simply not made accessible to other researchers' and is still construed 'as "unknown", "untested" or of questionable relevance or validity'. There are several important efforts to challenge such structures by the development of alternative South-South circuits of publication (e.g. the

Guadalajara International Book Fair, and alternative indexes such as SciELO and Latindex). Yet, while such circuits have clear de-colonizing potentials (Baraka Akilmali 2019), there is a risk that such efforts may create further divisions in the global knowledge production structures which do not challenge current patterns, or at least further strengthen ignorance in the Global North about the knowledge produced in the Global South (Baraka Akilmali 2019).

However, inequalities in the global economy of knowledge production are not evident only in terms of visibility and publications, but also and crucially in research funding. That current funding structures reproduce structural inequalities that systematically favour institutions in the Global North is something which has been highlighted, not the least, within development studies for a long time. While many DAC development aid donors are involved in supporting 'development relevant research' – largely in practical terms translated as being any phenomenon in the Global South – such funding is mainly provided for scholars in the Global North. Even research funding to 'strengthen research capacity' in partner countries in the South to a large extent benefits scholars in the Global North. This also includes multilateral funding schemes. A recent example of this, which made some African scholars write an open letter in *Nature Medicine*, was an initiative in 2017 by the United States, UK and Canada to collectively spend $1.1 billion on malaria including research funding, an initiative which left just 1 per cent of the funding to local in-country research institutions (Erondu et al. 2021). As highlighted in the Introduction, the project upon which this book is based reflects such inequalities in funding: it was funded by the Swedish Council, through Swedish development co-operation aid funds earmarked for scholars based in Sweden. While these Sweden-based scholars are encouraged to partner with researchers and institutions in the countries of research, the funding and project leader role must be managed by Swedish academics and universities.

Yet, in addition to these general inequalities in the global economy of knowledge production on the Global South, we believe that the silencing and exclusion of facilitating researchers described in this book also reflects how our identities 'are marked by the trace of the imperial pasts'. As described in various chapters of the book, facilitating researchers experience that contracting researchers at times perceive us/them and our/their lives as not deserving the same respect and protection as that of white contracting researchers. Moreover, as concluded in Chapter 1, classical colonial images of unreliability and lack of real commitment, including images of facilitating researchers 'as only interested in money', appear abound (Eriksson Baaz and Utas 2019; Mudinga 2020) among white contracting researchers. Contracting researchers, in many informal settings, share the view that 'you need to be present yourself, or have control mechanisms in place, to make sure data is collected properly'. This is based on the assumption that facilitating researchers cannot be trusted and may also fudge the data in some cases. We do not deny that such cases of inappropriate and unethical research practices occur. Yet, as is widely known, facilitating researchers alone do not commit data fraud and researchers in Europe and the United States have also been known to fabricate data and adopt unethical research methods and practices (Craig et al. 2020; Harvey 2020). Moreover, as this book demonstrates, contracting researchers show lack of integrity when they appropriate and claim research conducted by others. Blaming only facilitating researchers for fraud and research malpractices is thus both unfair and representative of long-standing racialized images of unreliable 'Others' (Eriksson Baaz 2005; Eriksson Baaz and Utas 2019). In short, the images that contracting researchers hold of themselves and facilitating researchers, and vice versa, which in turn are manifested in a research practice of mistrust, exclusion and silencing must at least in part be understood as shaped by the colonial pasts.

Hierarchies and inequalities in an increasingly marketized academia

Yet, the silencing and exclusion of facilitating researchers described in this book cannot simply be explained as a result of the lingering of colonial history and white identities of entitlement and superiority.

Such practices must also be placed within the hierarchical institutional context of academia itself and intersections between race, class and gender. As demonstrated in much research, academia remains a highly hierarchical institutional setting, systematically favouring some over others through race, class and gender – and their various intersectionalities (Arday and Mirza 2018; Delatolla et al. 2021; Mählck, Kusterer and Montgomery 2020; Mählck 2018; Schick 2000).

However, in addition to such clearly raced, classed and gendered inequalities academia is also a highly hierarchical setting, distinguishing between ranks (e.g. PhD students, post-doctoral, assistant professors, associate professors, full professors, chairs). The use and abuse of PhD students and other junior scholars (whatever background) by more senior staff in pursuit of furthering their own career ambitions is a well-known phenomenon. One example of this is PhD 'supervisors insisting their name goes on as a co-author when they've basically done their job, nothing more' (Macfarlane et al. 2017: 12). In short, the silencing and exclusion of facilitating researchers described in this book must also be situated in that context.

It must also be put in the context of academia as a highly competitive setting – and increasingly so it seems though progressive neo-liberalization/ marketization (Acker and Armenti 2004; Anderson et al. 2007; Chandler et al. 2002; Moosa 2018). Competition between researchers for funding, positions and publications has been increasingly perceived as a salutary driving force to enhanced knowledge. Over the last decades, academia has transformed into an a progressively competitive field: researchers' value is being measured in the number of publications and citations in high-ranked journals and they/we are constantly encouraged to act as entrepreneurs working to enhance our visibility and work on own brands. The pressure to publish has never been greater and even the academic language appears to have changed (e.g. more first-person expressions and more confident language) (Wheeler et al. 2021).

The negative effects of this trend are many and have been widely documented; increasing levels of stress; limited propensities to share information; mismanagement and fraudulent data management to produce positive results or path-breaking findings (as these increase publishing possibilities and citations); increasing strategic game-playing and even efforts to sabotage and defame others as well as other unethical and questionable research conduct (Acker and Armenti 2004; Anderson et al. 2007; Chandler et al. 2002; Moosa 2018). There seems to be an increasing trend of 'unethical authorship' (Herndon 2016; Isaila and Hostiuc 2019; Moosa 2018). Increased pressure to publish, in combination with the limited merits of articles with many co-authors, may also contribute to the reluctance to include facilitating researchers as co-authors.

As we will further develop below, there is no academic consensus about what merits co-authorship and views vary between fields. While co-authorship has long been the normal procedure in science, technology and medicine as a result of the working methods in these fields (e.g. labs involving many people) it has been rare in the humanities and social sciences, where academic writing previously has been seen as a solo activity, the outcome of the workings of one brilliant mind (Herndon 2016).

Yet, co-authorship has increased rapidly in the humanities and social sciences, in large due to the increasing pressure to publish, but also increasing co-operation in research (Macfarlane et al. 2017: 12). However, single authorship still holds high value in the humanities and social sciences and a large number of authors – as is common in science, technology and medicine – tend to be seen with suspicion and as attached with limited prestige (Herndon 2016). In short and given the increasing pressure to publish in order to access funding, positions and promotion – there is a strong pressure to publish – and with not too many co-authors. Hence, it is easy to see that such incentives can be manifested in 'unethical authorship' by excluding authors who would merit co-authorship but who do not possess the power to enforce authorship. A global survey with authors, reviewers and editors (yet, with a majority of respondents in the Europe and North America) conducted by the Taylor & Francis publishing group highlights a 'reality gap' in that authorship does not reflect the reality of the work put into the research and writing. The most glaring gap identified is that senior academics tend to be over-credited in authorships while junior academics are under-credited for the work that they do (Macfarlane et al. 2017). Hence, the silencing and exclusion of facilitating researchers described in this book must also be understood in relation to this general pattern in academia at large.

Let us now turn to the question of what needs to change and how. As mentioned initially, more research is clearly needed in order to assess the relative importance of different explanatory factors. Further knowledge about the role that institutional structures and norms within academia (and related institutions) play in the silencing and poor working conditions of facilitating researchers is needed – and will be explored further by the team. For instance: What role may limited knowledge/awareness of the realities of fieldwork, for instance among publishers, play in the continued silencing and poor working conditions of facilitating researchers? What relative role does prejudice against knowledge producers in the Global South play in the continued silencing and poor working conditions of facilitating researchers? What position do academic conventions (e.g. surrounding authorship and definitions of research ethics) play in the continued silencing and poor working conditions of facilitating researchers? What part do different national administrative rules and regulations (e.g. regulations around funding, remuneration and insurance) play in the continued silencing and poor working conditions of facilitating researchers?

Yet, inaction cannot be legitimized through the need to first provide better knowledge about the obstacles at play. In the below we will first account for what we believe needs to change, followed by suggestions on how we may bring change and the various actors that have to be involved.

What needs to change?[1]

Firstly, and most importantly, we call for truly collaborative approaches where the facilitating researchers are included throughout research projects cycles: from the outlining stage to the development of research questions, to the design of methodologies and researcher approaches, to analysis, all the way through the write-up and publication (see also Bisimwa Baganda 2019; Vogel and Musamba 2022). While such an inclusion can of course be achieved in different ways, it is difficult to imagine how it will be possible without changes in current unequal funding structures. As highlighted above, the systematic silencing, exclusion and even exploitation of facilitating researchers must fundamentally be understood as a reflection of the inequalities in the global economy of knowledge, when it comes to research funding. The current funding structures reproduce structural inequalities that systematically favour institutions and research agendas in the Global North. Unless this changes, it is difficult to imagine fundamental changes in research relations. We here choose to cite the authors of the Open Letter by African scholars mentioned above (Erondu et al. 2021):

For long-term progress, true partnerships and stronger collaborations, you, the funders, are responsible for totally transforming this model. We believe that in the same way we have to apply innovation in our work to fight diseases, innovation can be applied to the design of sustainable funding models with local researchers and organizations at their center.

Clearly, such changes in funding structures may not automatically lead to more visibility and power to facilitating researchers; especially given that exclusion and silencing of facilitating researchers also occur in national contexts, as highlighted in the book. Yet, it would by-pass one part in the funding chain (i.e. Northern-based universities) and thereby move the management closer to the context in which facilitating

---

[1] Parts of the following text have been previously published in blog form (see Abedi Dunia et al. 2019, 2020) and also appear in a joint article (see Abedi Dunia et al. 2023).

researchers work and as demonstrated in the book, some also already now act, at times, as national contracting researchers. Yet, even when holding such positions, we/they are often denied authorship.

Secondly, it has to be recognized that the contribution that many facilitating researchers make not only merits co-authorship, but also makes non-authorship by facilitating researchers both fraudulent and unethical – a 'brain theft' (see Bisimwa Baganda 2019). It must be acknowledged that recurrent ideas that facilitating researchers do not need to publish and/or that co-authorship in publications inevitably place facilitating researchers in danger are deeply problematic.

As highlighted earlier, there is no consensus about what merits co-authorship in the humanities and social sciences. The so-called Vancouver protocol, the guidelines of the International Committee of Medical Journal Editors,[2] which define the criteria for an authorship credit is often cited, but there is little comparable guidance for authorship in the humanities and social sciences (Macfarlane et al. 2017). A recent survey that adapted these principles to the humanities and social sciences field separated responsibilities meriting co-authorship into the following: (1) Being responsible for the conception and design of a project; (2) Being responsible for the analysis and/or interpretation of data; (3) Drafting the paper or revising it critically for intellectual content (Macfarlane et al. 2017).

As shown in the preceding chapters of the book, many facilitating researchers often play a crucial role in the first two phases. Recurrent arguments to delegitimize co-authorship in such cases are that they do not contribute to the writing process. Yet, how can you participate in something that you are not offered to be part of? The correct question should instead be: is it at all ethical to exclude facilitating researchers who have done the bulk of (1) and (2) above from (3)? This question

---

[2] According to this protocol, authorship requires: (1) Substantial contributions to the conception or design of the work; or the acquisition, analysis or interpretation of data for the work; (2) Drafting the work or revising it critically for important intellectual content; (3) Final approval of the version to be published, and agreement to be accountable for all aspects of the work in ensuring that questions related to the accuracy or integrity of any part of the work are appropriately investigated and resolved.

makes it very clear who decides. Importantly, facilitating researchers must not be denied co-authorship assuming that there is no role they play in theory building. The theory-data hierarchy is a deeply problematic current model of academic publications where theory building is attributed to Global North 'location' and labour, while empirical data collection is left to Global South researchers and is considered less important (Parashar 2021). Moreover, as highlighted in the book in the few cases when facilitating researchers are offered to provide inputs on research texts (and thereby possible co-authorship), texts are often sent without previous information and with such short notice that it is impossible for us/them to give feedback in time.

In a radical move to introduce transparency, accountability and integrity in research, the global medical journal *The Lancet* recently made the decision to reject papers on Africa which do not mention the role of African contributors and collaborators.[3] This is an excellent initiative in our view, but we also recognize that 'one size fits all' may not be applicable. Research is organized differently and contracting and facilitating researchers have different levels of independence and obligations depending on the disciplinary protocols they follow. Thus, it is hard to give up the concept of 'lone researchers' completely, only focusing on collaborations. Moreover, the problem with *The Lancet*'s policy is that the contribution of facilitating researchers could still go unrecognized, as authorship could be interpreted simply as the result on an enforced policy.

Thirdly, there is a need for a better and more transparent remuneration policy through clear contracts wherein the compensation is open for negotiation, rather than presented as a fixed fee, passed on informally by contracting researchers. Currently and as demonstrated in the book, many facilitating researchers fear that any attempt to renegotiate terms of compensation can result in the termination of the contract itself. This has to change so that the facilitating researchers

---

[3] https://www.universityworldnews.com/post.php?story=20220603115640789&fbclid=IwAR0ytWNQRe7IgmENjhPDmAyi18i6ntzgrAfyi72VmPN9ked5YqPes5x8Jss.

do not feel so disempowered. Moreover, and importantly and as is standard in many other contexts, remuneration has to reflect the level of risk. Relatedly, the current situation where facilitating researchers work without insurance and often have to cover unexpected costs in the field – caused by accidents, illnesses, theft, and managing intimidation and threats – through the meagre remuneration is untenable. We need to arrange for access to insurance through formal institutions, as is standard for contracting researchers. Yet, until this is possible, funds must cover unexpected costs crucial to the health, wellbeing and safety of facilitating researchers within overall project budgets.

Finally, we believe that we need to move towards less physical presence of contracting researchers in data collection at 'field sites'. Decreasing travelling of contracting researchers is, as mentioned in Chapter 1, warranted given the need to combat climate (Higham and Font 2020; Nevins, Allen and Watson 2022) and will hopefully be considered as a crucial aspect of research ethics in the future. Yet, in addition to mitigating climate change, more limited physical presence of contracting researchers in data collection may also revisit the roles and responsibilities as well as the acknowledgement of facilitating researchers, and the labour they perform. The Covid pandemic has already set the trend in this regard as it immobilized Global North researchers and restricted travels globally, leading to a potential reassessment of roles of facilitating researchers located in the Global South in many contexts (see Abedi Dunia et al. 2023; Bisoka 2020; Mwambari, Purdeková and Bisoka 2021; Myrttinen and Mastonshoeva 2019). We are not suggesting that contracting researchers based in the Global North should never travel for fieldwork. We also recognize that fieldwork visits and collaboration can have their own dynamics that can suffer if all the research is carried out by only one side. There is much to learn from collaborative fieldwork that can enrich and enhance the knowledge that is being produced in the social sciences. Yet, revisiting travel policies for research is a must to address urgent environment and climate change issues and can also contribute to a change in power dynamics between facilitating and contracting researchers.

Agents responsible for change?

Clearly and as history so astutely demonstrates, change requires much more than appealing to the willingness or consciousness of individual researchers. The interviews and discussions with contracting researchers conducted within the project also underscored this. Many contracting researchers when being asked about the reasons for the state of the art explained that they simply follow traditional arrangements ('i.e. we just do and pay as others have done before us'). Yet, many also mentioned incentive structures within academia for instance related to authorship merits, as well as the workings of various institutions, such as publishers and research funding bodies not asking questions about the role of facilitating researchers. In short, a more comprehensive approach in which various institutions and crucial actors take responsibility and press for change in practices and current incentive structures is needed.

Firstly, funding agencies and ethics board and committees assessing research projects must play a vital role. In addition to the need to alter current unequal funding structures highlighted above, funders of research as well as ethic review boards need to ask questions about the role and situation of facilitating researchers before approving any funding or ethics clearance. In order for this to be effective, there also needs to be a follow-up upon the completion of research projects, backed up by testifying documents from the concerned facilitating researchers. Such institutions need to start to ask questions such as: What will be the research process? Even if the application does not recognize inputs from facilitating researchers, can one assume that the research can be successfully completed without facilitating research inputs? Where 'local researchers' and 'local assistants' are mentioned what specific roles and responsibilities are assigned to them and do they have any inputs in the proposal and budgetary allocation? Is there a fair compensation model for 'local researchers' in the proposed budget which also covers insurance? What decisions have been taken regarding authorship of final outputs? These questions will require evidence from facilitating researchers as well.

Secondly, academic publishers, in particular academic journals, along with funding agencies and ethics review boards have a great responsibility and role to play in effectuating change. They need to introduce accountability and transparency by asking questions about the research process and the role of facilitating researchers. Details about how the project was conducted, how co-authorship was decided (or not), what remunerations were offered to facilitating researchers need to be asked as part of the review process of submitted publications. Vague and passive formulations (e.g. 'I', 'we', 'with a team of assistants') need to be investigated, along with claims of teamwork, and roles of team members especially in data collection and analysis. There needs to be further questioning of who was involved in the writing process and who was excluded and if that was a fair process. Is it reasonable to assume that a single authored article or book from Global North researchers that uses empirical material from the Global South did not include the labour of facilitating researchers from the Global South? If not, more questions have to be asked.

Ideally, testifying documentation should be asked from facilitating researchers, specifying their contribution – particularly if not included as co-writers. How to practically achieve this, is of course not an easy question and there is a clear risk that such procedures will not solve the problem. Yet, the survey conducted by Macfarlane et al. (2017) found that most journal editors state that they are prepared to intervene if they believe that there are signs of 'unethical authorship' more generally (e.g. between senior and junior scholars), which is at least a promising start. As alluded to above, one reason why questions are rarely asked now by publishers and editors may be a limited knowledge of how fieldwork in insecure settings really looks like and the indispensable role that facilitating researchers play.

Yet, while change requires much more than appealing to the willingness or consciousness of individual researchers, we can also do much more as individual researchers. In addition to making our own research practice more ethical, we/they can also put pressure on fellow colleagues through constructive critique and engagement. In particular, those of us who act as reviewers have a special responsibility as reviewers of journal articles and research applications. As part of the review process, we must demand clarity about the research process and role of facilitating researchers, in any fieldwork-based project, article or book (see questions above).

Finally, facilitating researchers our/them-selves clearly also have an important role to play. One such possible route is the formation of union-like organizations. One of the obstacles identified in workshops and highlighted in the book is the high competition between and the lack of organization among facilitating researchers. This, in turn, makes it possible for contracting researchers to haggle by referring to other facilitating researchers willing to do the work for less remuneration. While not an easy task, creating union-type organizations could be a useful way to negotiate better pay, demand co-authorship and assurances of security measures, and in general assert greater authority rather than 'merely limiting our/them-selves to footnotes'. Such organizations could also be useful in enhancing research capacity by sharing experiences and arranging seminars. In addition to this, the yearly organization of conferences, seminars or symposia for facilitating researchers could help enhance collaboration and further knowledge about how various research institutions work. Common platforms and learning could empower facilitating researchers to break the silence, voice our/their experiences at various levels and carve out demands that protect our/their rights and concerns.

Foreclosing possible objections

Given the somewhat sensitive topic of this book, we foresee objections of various sorts. We have also encountered such objections in relation to different presentations we have had related to the book. Interestingly, much of this concerns the recommendations related to co-authorship. One of the objections here has been: '*but not all facilitating researcher tasks merit co-authorship. Do you suggest that people who act as a driver but also locate some respondents are to be a co-author?'* We are not of the view that all facilitating researcher tasks should be considered for co-authorship, and we believe that facilitating researchers may also not think of that as the most desirable outcome. However, it is important for facilitating researchers to be offered the opportunity to become co-authors, especially if they have been involved in adapting methodology to the context, data collection and analysis. Moreover, as has been highlighted in the previous chapters above (see also Mudinga 2020), we strongly advice against the tendency to refuse co-authorship, out of security concerns of the facilitating researchers. All of the facilitating researchers who co-authored this book clearly feel that they are capable to assess such risks our/themselves.

Another objection that we received is *'well, this is easy for you to say who are senior researchers, but what about junior scholars and PhD students'*; (the 'you' here referring to Eriksson Baaz, Parashar and Utas who hold full professorships). This is a truly valid point, and we would like to emphasize the responsibility especially of senior scholars. Clearly, it is for instance, more difficult for PhD scholars due to the general rules of co-authorship in order to be accepted as a successful PhD holder. Until/when this changes, we would encourage PhD scholars, when applicable, to better and duly acknowledge the crucial role of facilitating researchers in other parts of the thesis (methodology sections, etc.) and not simply reduce the contribution to short phrases in acknowledgement sections. Telling a more true story of how field research is conducted is crucial in order to enhance knowledge about the vital contribution of facilitating researchers.

Another objection often received is *'well, not just contracting researchers based in the Global North engage in exploitative research behaviour, actually "we" (here read: Global North researchers) treat them better than researchers based in the Global South'*. As acknowledged and demonstrated in the book, exploitative research behaviour is also prevalent among more privileged researchers in and of the 'Global South'. Yet, that fact does not absolve anyone from responsibility and debates on who is better or worse are truly futile (and appear slightly juvenile).

Importantly though, our call for ethical research behaviour and recognizing privilege goes beyond simple North/South divisions and binaries of good/bad, racist/non-racist. It is absolutely essential to acknowledge that even so-called critical and postcolonial scholars, and privileged researchers in the Global South, are often implicated in exploitative practices. In short, we all have to remain hyper-vigilant about our own positionality and complicity.

A further objection we heard – relating more to the practical suggestions – is that: *'these suggestions provide too much power to facilitating researchers who can insist on being co-authors even though they have done very little work. They could even untruthfully complain about remuneration and other aspects for their own benefit.'* Such objections in part reflect, rather problematic stereotypes and fears of being used among contracting researchers (see Chapter 1 and Eriksson Baaz and Utas 2019). They also fail to acknowledge the continued inequalities in power and resources. Given the pervasive nature of existing inequalities, the greatest risk is that facilitating researchers (with the implementation of new standards) will still not be able or willing to claim our/their rights, as this might adversely affect our/their livelihood opportunities. Moreover, if some would attempt to 'unfairly' use ethical standards to their own benefit, the magnitude of this would be incomparable to the long-standing unfair silencing and exploitation embedded in North-South knowledge production.

We hope that our anticipation of the immediate objections to rectify things will enable further debate and reflection. Our suggestions of how we may move things forward are not set in stone and certainly not complete. If research ethics and human rights are to be taken seriously, we must all bear responsibility and work for transformatory changes to make fieldwork a non-exploitative experience in collaborative knowledge production.

References

Abedi Dunia, O., Eriksson Baaz, M., Parashar, S., Toppo, A.O.M., Utas, M., and Vincent, J. (2023), 'Visibilising hidden realities and uncertainties: The "post-covid" move towards decolonized and ethical field research practices', *International Journal of Science and Research Methodology*. DOI: 10.1080/13645579.2023.2173427

Acker, S., and Armenti, C. (2004), 'Sleepless in academia', *Gender and Education*, 16(1): 3–24.

Adedi D., O., Bisimwa, S. E., Cirhuza, E., Eriksson Baaz, M., Ferekani, J., Imili, P., Kambale, E., Mapatano, J., Mulimbi, L., Mukungilwa, B., Mukingi, L., Mwambari, D., Parashar, S., Rukanyaga Assumani, D., Sinzaher, W., Utas, M., and Vincent, J. (October 22, 2019), 'Moving out of the backstage: How can we decolonize research?', *The Disorder of Things*. Available online: https://thedisorderofthings.com/2019/10/22/moving-out-of-the-backstage-how-canwe-decolonize-research/

Adedi D., O., Eriksson Baaz, M., Mwambari, D., Parashar, S., Toppo, A. O. M., and Vincent, J. B.M. (2020), 'The covid-19 opportunity: Creating more ethical and sustainable research practices', Items, Insights from the Social Sciences, the Social Science Research Council, New York.

Anderson, M. S., Ronning, E. A., De Vries, R., and Martinson, B. C. (2007), 'The perverse effects of competition on scientists' work and relationships', *Science and Engineering Ethics*, 13(4): 437–61.

Arday, J., and Mirza, H. S. (eds.) (2018), *Dismantling Race in Higher Education: Racism, Whiteness and Decolonising the Academy*, London: Palgrave Macmillan.

Baraka Akilmali, J. (2019), 'Escaping Big Brother's gaze in research in the Global South'. Available online: https://www.gicnetwork.be/bukavu-series-escaping-big-brothers-gaze-in-research-in-the-global-south/

Bisimwa Baganda, S. (2019), '"They stole his brain": The local researcher – a data collector, or researcher in his own right?"', Blog for Silent Voices, Bukavu Series. Available online: https://www.gicnetwork.be/bukavu-series-they-stole-his-brain-the-local-researcher-a-data-collector-or-researcher-in-his-own-right/

Bisoka, A.N. (2020). "Disturbing the Aesthetics of Power: Why Covid-19 Is Not an "Event" for Fieldwork-based Social Scientists", Items, Insights from the Social Sciences, the Social Science Research Council, New York. https://items.ssrc.org/covid-19-and-the-social-sciences/social-research-and-insecurity/disturbing-the-aesthetics-of-power-why-covid-19-is-not-an-event-for-fieldwork-based-social-scientists/

Björkman, L. (2021), *Bombay Brokers*, Durham: Duke University Press.

Bliesemann de Guevara, B., and Bøås, M. (eds.) (2020), *Doing Fieldwork in Areas of International Intervention: A Guide to Research in Violent and Closed Contexts*, Bristol: Bristol University Press.

Bloor, M., Fincham, B., and Sampson, H. (2010), 'Unprepared for the worst: Risk of harm for qualitative researchers', *Methodological Innovations Online*, 5(1): 45–55.

Bøås, M. (2020), 'Unequal research relationships in highly insecure places: Of fear, funds and friendship', in Berit Bliesemann de Guevara and Morten Bøås (eds.) *Doing Fieldwork in Areas of International Intervention: A Guide to Research in Violent and Closed Contexts*: 61–72. Bristol: Bristol University Press, Digital.

Borpujari, P. (2019), 'The problem with "fixers"', *Columbia Journalism Review*. Available online: https://www.cjr.org/special_report/fixers.php

Buhendwa Nshobole, J. (2020), '"Donor-Researchers' and Recipient-Researchers": Bridging the gap between researchers from the Global North and Global South"', Blog for Silent Voices, Bukavu Series. Available online: https://www.gicnetwork.be/donor-researchers-and-recipient-researchers-bridging-the-gap-between-researchers-from-the-global-north-and-global-south/

Chandler, J., Barry, J., and Clark, H. (2002), 'Stressing academe: The wear and tear of the new public management', *Human Relations*, 55(9): 1051–69.

Cirhuza, E. (2019), 'Remunerating researchers from the Global South: A source of academic prostitution?', Blog for Silent Voices, Bukavu Series. Available online: https://www.gicnetwork.be/bukavu-series-remunerating-researchers-from-the-global-south-a-source-of-academic-prostitution/

Cirhuza, E. (2020), 'Taken out of the picture? The researcher from the Global South and the fight against "academic neo-colonialism"', Blog for Silent Voices, Bukavu Series. Available online: https://www.gicnetwork.be/taken-out-of-the-picture-the-researcher-from-the-global-south-and-the-fight-against-academic-neo-colonialism/

Cirhuza, É., and Kadetwa Kayanga, E. (2020), 'In the presence of "whiteskin": The challenges of expectations upon encountering white researchers', Blog for Silent Voices, Bukavu Series. Available online: https://www.gicnetwork.be/in-the-presence-of-white-skin-the-challenges-of-expectations-upon-encountering-white-researchers/

Clauset, A., Arbesman, S., and Larremore, D. B. (2015), 'Systematic inequality and hierarchy in faculty hiring networks', *Science Advances*, 1(1): e1400005.

Collyer, F. M. (2018), 'Global patterns in the publishing of academic knowledge: Global North, Global South', *Current Sociology*, 66(1): 56–73.

Cons, J. (2014), 'Field dependencies: Mediation, addiction and anxious fieldwork at the India-Bangladesh border', *Ethnography*, 15(3): 375–93. doi:10.1177/1466138114533457

Craig, R., Cox, A., Tourish, D., and Thorpe, A. (2020), 'Using retracted journal articles in psychology to understand research misconduct in the social sciences: What is to be done?' *Research Policy*, 49(4): 103930.

Cronin-Furman, K., and Lake, M. (2018), 'Ethics abroad: Fieldwork in fragile and violent contexts', *PS: Political Science & Politics*: 1–8.

Dar, S., and Ibrahim, Y. (2019), 'The blackened body and white governmentality: Managing the UK academy and the production of shame', *Gender, Work & Organization*, 26(9): 1241–54.

De Jong, S. (2018), 'Brokerage and transnationalism: Present and past intermediaries, social mobility, and mixed loyalties', *Identities*, 25(5), 610–28.

Deane, K., and Stevano, S. (2016), 'Towards a political economy of the use of research assistants: Reflections from fieldwork in Tanzania and Mozambique', *Qualitative Research*, 16(2): 213–28. doi:10.1177/1468794115578776

Delatolla et al. (2021), 'Challenging institutional racism in international relations and our profession: Reflections, experiences, and strategies', *Millennium*, 50(1): 110–48.

Eriksson Baaz, M. (2005), *The Paternalism of Partnership: A Postcolonial Reading of Identity in Development Aid*, London & New York: Zed Books.

Eriksson Baaz, M., and Utas, M. (2019), 'Exploring the backstage: Methodological and ethical issues surrounding the role of research brokers in insecure zones', *Civil Wars*, 21(2): 157–78. doi:10.1080/13698249.2019.1656357

Erondu, N. A., Aniebo, I., Kyobutungi, C., Midega, J., Okiro, E., and Okumu, F. (2021), 'Open letter to international funders of science and development in Africa', *Nature Medicine*, 27(5): 742–4.

Gikandi, S. (1996), *Maps of Englishness: Writing Identity in the Culture of Colonialism*, by Simon Gikandi. New York: Columbia University Press.

Griaule, M. (1948), *Dieu d'eau, entretiens avec Ogotemmeli*, Paris: Editions du Chene.

Grimm, J., Koehler, K., Lust, E. M., Saliba, I., and Schierenbeck, I. (2020), *Safer Field Research in the Social Sciences: A Guide to Human and Digital*

Security in Hostile Environments, London, California, New Delhi, Singapore: Sage.

Grindal, B. T., and Salamone, F. A. (1995), *Bridges to Humanity: Narratives on Anthropology and Friendship*, Prospect Heights, IL: Waveland Press.

Gupta, A. (2014), 'Authorship, research assistants and the ethnographic field', *Ethnography*, 15(3): 394–400. doi:10.1177/1466138114533460

Harvey, L. (2020), 'Research fraud: A long-term problem exacerbated by the clamour for research grants', *Quality in Higher Education*, 26(3): 243–61.

Herndon, N. C. (2016), 'Research fraud and the publish or perish world of academia', *Journal of Marketing Channels*, 23(3): 91–6.

Higham, J., and Font, X. (2020), 'Decarbonising academia: Confronting our climate hypocrisy', *Journal of Sustainable Tourism*, 28(1): 1–9.

Hirblinger, A. T., and Simons, C. (2015), 'The good, the bad, and the powerful: Representations of the "Local" in peacebuilding', *Security Dialogue*, 46(5): 422–39.

Hoffman, K. (2014), *Caught between Apprehension and Comprehension: Dilemmas of Immersion in a Conflict Setting*, Retrieved from Copenhagen: https://www.files.ethz.ch/isn/186271/wp_2014-09.pdf

Hoffman, D., and Tarawalley, M. (2014), 'Frontline collaborations: The research relationship in unstable places', *Ethnography*, 15(3): 291–310. doi:10.1177/1466138114533463

Hoover Green, A., and Cohen, D. K., 'Centering human subjects: The ethics of "desk research" on political violence', *Journal of Global Security Studies*, 6(2), June 2021.

Isaila, O., and Hostiuc, S. (2019), 'Plagiarism in scientific articles. A brief review', *Journal of Intercultural Management and Ethics*, 2(2): 47–51.

Jabri, V. (2013), Peacebuilding, the local and the international: A colonial or a postcolonial rationality? *Peacebuilding*, 1(1): 3–16.

Jenkins, S. A. (2015), 'Assistants, guides, collaborators, friends: The concealed figures of conflict research', *Journal of Contemporary Ethnography*, 47(2): 143–70. doi:10.1177/0891241615619993

Käihkö, I. (2019), 'On brokers, commodification of information and Liberian Former Combatants', *Civil Wars*, 21(2): 179–99. doi:10.1080/13698249.2019.1602806

Kovats-Bernat, J. C. (2002), 'Negotiating dangerous fields: Pragmatic strategies for fieldwork amid violence and terror', *American Anthropologist*, 104(1): 208–22. doi:10.1525/aa.2002.104.1.208

Macfarlane, B., Devine, E., Drake, T., Gilbert, A., Robinson, M., and White, I. (2017), 'Co-authorship in humanities and the social sciences: A global view', Taylor & Francis Group. Available online: http://authorservices.taylorandfrancis

Mählck, P. (2018), 'Racism, precariousness and resistance: Development-aid-funded PhD training in Sweden', *Postcolonial Directions in Education*, 7(1): 11–36.

Mählck, P., Kusterer, H. L., and Montgomery, H. (2020), 'What professors do in peer review: Interrogating assessment practices in the recruitment of professors in Sweden', *Gender, Work & Organization*, 27(6): 1361–77.

Mapatano, J. (2019), 'When you become Pombe Yangu (My Beer): Dealing with the financial expectations of research participants', Blog for Silent Voices, Bukavu Series. Available online: https://www.gicnetwork.be/when-you-become-pombe-yangu-my-beer-dealing-with-the-financial-expectations-of-research-participants/

Middleton, T., and Cons, J. (2014), 'Coming to terms: Reinserting research assistants into ethnography's past and present', *Ethnography*, 15(3): 279–90. doi:10.1177/1466138114533466

Middleton, T., and Pradhan, E. (2014), 'Dynamic duos: On partnership and the possibilities of postcolonial ethnography', *Ethnography*, 15(3): 355–74. doi:10.1177/1466138114533451

Molony, T., and Hammett, D. (2007), 'The friendly financier: Talking money with the silenced assistant', *Human Organization*, 66(3): 292–300. doi:10.17730/humo.66.3.74n7x53x7r40332h

Moosa, I. A. (2018), *Publish or Perish: Perceived Benefits versus Unintended Consequences*, Cheltenham, UK: Edward Elgar Publishing Ltd.

Mudinga, E. (2020), 'We barely know these researchers from the South! Reflections on problematic assumptions about local research collaborators', Blog for Silent Voices, Bukavu Series. Available online: https://www.gicnetwork.be/we-barely-know-these-researchers-from-the-south-reflections-on-problematic-assumptions-about-local-research-collaborators/

Mukungilwa, B. (2019), '"These Phantom Researchers": What of their visibility in academic publications?' Blog for Silent Voices, Bukavu Series. Available online: https://www.gicnetwork.be/these-phantom-researchers-what-of-their-visibility-in-academic-publications/

Murrell, C. (2015), *Foreign Correspondents and International Newsgathering: The Role of Fixers*, New York: Routledge.

Mwambari, D., and Owor, A. (2019), 'The black market of knowledge production', *Governance in Conflict Network (blog)*, 20.

Mwambari, D., Purdeková, A., and Bisoka, A. N. (2021), 'Covid-19 and research in conflict-affected contexts: Distanced methods and the digitalisation of suffering', *Qualitative Research*, 0(0).

Myrttinen, H., and Mastonshoeva, S. (2019), 'From remote control to collaboration: Conducting NGO research at a distance in Tjikistan', *Civil Wars*, 21(2): 228–48.

Nevins, J., Allen, S., and Watson, M. (2022), 'A path to decolonization? Reducing air travel and resource consumption in higher education', *Travel Behaviour and Society*, 26: 231–9.

Nordstrom, C. (1997), *A Different Kind of War Story*, Philadelphia: University of Pennsylvania Press.

Palmer, L. (2018), 'Being the bridge: News fixers' perspectives on reporting the war on terror', *Journalism*, 19(3): 314–32.

Palmer, L. (2019), *The Fixers. Local News Workers and the Underground Labor of International Reporting*, Oxford: Oxford University Press.

Parashar, S. (2017), 'Beyond the "Case for Colonialism": Rethinking academic practices and dissent', *The Disorder Of Things*. Available online: https://thedisorderofthings.com/2017/10/08/beyond-the-case-for-colonialism-rethinking-academic-practices-and-dissent/

Parashar, S. (2019), 'Research brokers, researcher identities and affective performances: The inside/outsider conundrum', *Civil Wars*, 21(2): 249–70.

Parashar, S. (2021), 'Racialising the 'Field': Global South as 'Case Study' in Delatolla A, Rahman M, Anand D, et al. Challenging institutional racism in international relations and our profession: Reflections, experiences and strategies. *Millennium*, 2021; 50(1): 110–148.

Peter, M., and Strazzari, F. (2017), 'Securitisation of research: Fieldwork under new restrictions in Darfur and Mali', *Third World Quarterly*, 38(7): 1531–50. doi:10.1080/01436597.2016.1256766

Plaut, S., and Klein, P. (2019), '"Fixing" the journalist-fixer relationship: A critical look towards developing best practices in global reporting', *Journalism Studies*, 20(12): 1696–713.

Powdermaker, H. (1966), *Stranger and Friend: The Way of an Anthropologist*, New York: W. W. Norton.

Sabaratnam, M. (2013), 'Avatars of Eurocentrism in the critique of the liberal peace', *Security Dialogue*, 44(3): 259–78.

Sangarasivam, Y. (2001), 'Researcher, Informant, "Assassin," Me', *Geographical Review*, 91(1/2): 95–104. doi:10.2307/3250809

Sanjek, R. (1993), 'Anthropology's hidden colonialism: Assistants and their ethnographers', *Anthropology Today*, 9(2): 13–18. doi:10.2307/2783170

Schick, C. (2000), 'Keeping the ivory tower white: Discourses of racial domination', *Canadian Journal of Law & Society/La Revue Canadienne Droit et Société*, 15(2): 70–90.

Spivak, G. C. (1988), 'Can the subaltern speak?', in C. Nelson and L. Grossberg (eds.), *Marxism and the Interpretation of Cultures*, Urbana: University of Illinois.

Sukarieh, M., and Tannock, S. (2019), 'Subcontracting academia: Alienation, exploitation and disillusionment in the UK overseas Syrian refugee research industry', *Antipode*, 51(2): 664–80.

Thamani Mwaka, P. (2019), 'Waiting for the morning birds: Researcher trauma in insecure environments', Blog for Silent Voices, Bukavu Series. Available online: https://www.gicnetwork.be/bukavu-series-waiting-for-the-morning-birds-researcher-trauma-in-insecure-environments/

Themner, A. (2022), 'On brokers, biases and leaving the Veranda: Working with research brokers in political science based field research', *Civil Wars*: 1–23.

Turner, S. (2013), 'The silenced research assistant speaks her mind', in S. Turner (ed.), *Red Stamps and Gold Stars: Fieldwork Dilemmas in Upland Socialist Asia*, Copenhagen: NIAS Press.

Turner, V. W. (1967), *The Forest of Symbols: Aspects of Ndembu Ritual*, Ithaca, NY: Cornell University Press.

Utas, M. (2019), 'Research brokers we use and abuse while researching civil wars and their aftermaths – methodological concerns', *Civil Wars*, 21(2): 271–85. doi:10.1080/13698249.2019.1654325

Vlassenroot, K. (2006), 'War and social research: The limits of empirical methodologies in war-torn environments', *Civilisations*, 54: 191–8.

Vogel, C., and Musamba, J. (2022), 'Towards a politics of collaborative worldmaking: Ethics, epistemologies and mutual positionalities in conflict research', *Ethnography*: 14661381221090895.

Wheeler, M. A., Vylomova, E., McGrath, M. J., and Haslam, N. (2021), 'More confident, less formal: Stylistic changes in academic psychology writing from 1970 to 2016', *Scientometrics*, 126(12): 9603–12.

Zambrana, R. E., Harvey Wingfield, A., Lapeyrouse, L. M., Dávila, B. A., Hoagland, T. L., and Valdez, R. B. (2017), 'Blatant, subtle, and insidious: URM faculty perceptions of discriminatory practices in predominantly White institutions', *Sociological Inquiry*, 87(2): 207–32.

Index

academic publishers 5, 24, 161, 171–2
academic research/researchers 4, 10, 16–17, 27, 32, 37, 41, 47–8, 98, 102, 117, 133, 145, 147, 161, 163–6, 171
Adivasis (indigenous people) of Jharkhand 17, 43, 45–6, 66, 71–3, 71 n.1, 81, 84, 109, 118–20, 122, 129, 131–2, 155
    Adivasi women 73, 81, 118–20, 131
Africa/African 89, 137, 152, 162, 167, 169
anthropology 9–10, 32
apprenticeships 91
armed conflicts 2–3, 17–18, 22, 27, 93, 102–7, 109–11. *See also* conflict dynamics; insecurities of facilitating researchers, risks/risky environments
armed groups 17, 47–9, 53–4, 58, 87, 102–4, 106, 108. *See also* Naxalites/Naxalite movement
authorship 130, 161, 165–6, 168–9, 168 n.2, 171. *See also* co-authorship

Baaz, Eriksson 5–6, 160, 174
Barla, Dayamani 73
bilateral development cooperation 47–8, 98, 146. *See also* multilateral development cooperation
black market 14–15. *See also specific concepts*
brokers (brokering researchers) 7–8, 10, 20, 22–4, 27
budgets, research projects 5, 40, 48, 94–5, 103, 115, 128–9, 170–1

CARE organization 40
caste 119, 122, 130
Children Associated with the War (CAW) project 34
CIDA organization 40
civil war. *See* Sierra Leone (research during civil war)
class 18, 39, 119, 122, 124, 157, 164
climate change 11, 170
co-authorship 6, 19, 21, 24, 64, 74, 77–8, 87, 89, 108, 145, 158, 164–5, 168–9, 173–5
collaboration, research 3, 5, 30, 41, 85, 88, 121–2, 145, 148, 152, 167, 169–70, 173, 175
Collyer, F. M. 161
colonial/colonialism 13, 15, 23, 40, 118, 147, 160–3
commercialization 27, 47
commissioning researchers. *See* contracting researchers
compensation for facilitating research 24, 54–5, 65, 67, 128, 169, 171
conflict dynamics 10, 13, 16–17, 26–7, 49, 63, 66, 86, 98, 101–5, 110–11, 134. *See also* armed conflicts
Cons, J. 13
consultancy/consultants 27, 32, 36–7, 69, 137, 144–6
contracting researchers 2, 4, 6–10, 14, 17–18, 20–3, 25 n.1, 28, 32, 37, 49, 51–2, 54, 56–7, 59, 63, 66–9, 83, 92, 94–7, 99, 105–9, 119, 158, 160, 163. *See also* facilitating researchers
    benefits of working with qualified/experienced 8, 36, 40–2, 45, 48

184 Index

broken promises of 21, 72, 74
on feedback/job (work) opportunities/remuneration 75–80, 97, 113–16, 121, 124–7, 159–60
to local community 80–2
Covid-19 pandemic restrictions 11
facilitators's positive experiences with 140–2, 152–6, 160 (*see also* Sierra Leone, positive experiences of facilitator-contractor)
false accusations on facilitators 79
from Global North 2, 7, 22–3, 25 n.1, 26, 29, 42, 96, 115, 117, 136–7, 146, 170, 174
insurance for working in conflict zones 98
kidnapping of (in dangerous zones) 103
non-recognition of facilitators 6, 43–5, 66–7, 72, 74, 85–92
pride for working with white 39, 155
racial discrimination by 41
research relations with facilitators 13–14, 31–6, 42, 75–7, 79, 123, 133
as risk 105–9, 159
safety of 12–13, 28–9, 38, 101, 105, 147, 158–9
sexual harassment from 128–9
unethical standards of 24, 75, 77, 82, 112, 114, 120–4, 126, 163, 165, 168, 172
ungrateful attitude of 67–8, 74, 106
Covid-19 pandemic 5, 11, 15, 73, 170
CRS organization 40

DANIDA organization 40
data-collection/research settings 2, 6, 8–9, 11, 13, 21, 43, 51–2, 54–5, 59–62, 71, 76, 78, 85–6, 88, 95, 98–9, 102–3, 123, 169–70. *See also* fieldwork practices
interpretation and translation of 21, 29, 43, 57–8, 62–4, 130, 158, 168, 168 n.2
misrepresentation of data 129–32, 165
Democratic Republic of the Congo (DRC) 2, 5, 8, 15, 17–19, 21–3, 51–2, 72–3, 93, 109, 113–15, 117
Bukavu 55, 59–60
data collection
challenges during 59–62
interpretation and translation of 62–4
Goma 55, 59–60
identifying research respondents 57–9
non-recognition of facilitators 85–90
North Kivu 49
positive experiences of facilitators-contractors 152–3
post-fieldwork 64–5
preparation of questionnaires/interview guides 57–9
research funding 132–3
research networks, benefits and drawbacks of 47–9, 132–5
risky environments (inter-community riots) at 53–4
travel planning/meeting arrangements 52–7
diverse/diversity 16, 18, 20, 26, 33, 73, 75, 119, 121, 157
donor institutions 40, 146, 162. *See also specific institutions*
Dunia, Abedi 4–5, 9, 19, 47

Ebola crises 27, 33, 37
education, facilitating researchers 14, 16–18, 26, 34, 37–40, 43–5, 88, 137, 144–5, 151, 154, 157

employment(s) 14, 36–7, 43–9, 109
ethic review boards 24, 171–2
ethnicity 17–18, 28, 49, 52, 61, 132
European Union (EU) 40
Europe/European 11, 16, 32, 34–5, 41–2, 59–60, 62, 89, 121, 132–3, 146–7, 163, 166
exploitation/exploitative relations 2, 7, 10–11, 18–19, 23, 30, 38, 43, 45, 47, 75, 77, 80, 91, 97, 109, 112, 117–20, 122–3, 128, 137, 160, 174–5

facilitating researchers
  additional costs during fieldwork 98–103
  challenges during data collection 59–62
  changes for inclusion throughout research projects 167–70
    agents responsible for change 171–3
  core committee 122–3
  facilitating-contracting research relations 13–14, 31–6, 42, 123, 133 (*see also* contracting researchers)
    bitter experiences with contractors 75–7, 79–80, 84, 86, 110, 114–15, 121, 125–6, 128–9, 131
    long-term relationships 141–3, 151
    positive experiences with contractors 140–2, 152–6, 160 (*see also* Sierra Leone, positive experiences of facilitator-contractor)
  false accusations by contractors 79
  fear of opposing contractors 83–4
  formal research training 45
  growth and academic careers 74
  insecurities of (*see* insecurities of facilitating researchers)
  insurance (inaccessible) 13, 40, 48, 60, 98–9, 159, 166, 170–1
  local assistants/researchers 7–8, 48, 66–7, 70, 75, 91–2, 131, 133, 136–7, 161, 171
  local knowledge of 28, 35–6, 44, 47, 77, 129, 139
  payments/salaries (*see* remuneration)
  post-fieldwork 64–5
  recognition, lack of 6, 43–5, 66–7, 72, 74, 85–92, 132, 169
  research networks, benefits and drawbacks of 47–9, 132–5
  responsibilities of 5, 11–13, 18, 24, 27–31, 38, 43–4, 52–3, 61–2, 104–5, 109, 129, 158, 173
  rights of 38–9 (*see also* education, facilitating researchers)
  roles of 7–8, 10–12, 19–21, 23–4, 29, 44, 48, 51–2, 63–4, 71, 168, 172–3 (*see also specific roles*)
  subcontracting 90, 95
  women in facilitating research (*see* women in facilitating research)
favouritisms 134
fieldwork practices 3, 9–10, 13–14, 32, 34, 42, 44, 48, 51, 77–8, 85, 95–7, 121, 124, 137, 147. *See also* data-collection/research settings; Democratic Republic of the Congo (DRC); Jharkhand, India; Sierra Leone
  additional costs during 98–103
  conflict-related risks 103–5, 110
fixers 7, 35
funding agencies 24, 171–2. *See also specific organizations*

gender 17–18, 20, 33, 37, 73–4, 92, 129–30, 137, 164
  gender equality 73, 119

Global North 2, 4, 7, 11, 22–3, 25 n.1, 26, 29, 32, 42, 88, 96, 115, 117–18, 136–7, 146, 149, 161–2, 169–70, 172, 174–5
Global South 3–4, 7, 11, 18, 23, 29, 41, 88, 118, 149, 160–2, 169–70, 172, 174–5
Great Lakes 49

hierarchy 119, 123, 163–6
high-profile researchers/projects 32, 43, 47, 68, 77, 110, 117–18, 120, 130
hospitality of local people 67–8, 81–2, 111
humanitarian agency. *See specific organizations*
humanities 165, 168

incentives (lack of) 75, 95, 98–103, 165, 171. *See also* remuneration
India 4, 15–16, 18–19, 21–3, 32, 34, 85, 91–2, 117–18, 122–3, 133, 136
  broker in 8
  Jharkhand (*see* Jharkhand, India)
  Naxalites/Naxalite movement in 18, 66, 73, 73 n.2
  remote research practices in 155
  Scheduled Tribes (STs) 71 n.1
  social structure in 119
inequalities between researchers. *See* unequal relations in research process
informants 9, 21, 45, 58, 63, 90, 102, 111, 158
insecurities of facilitating researchers 3–4, 9, 12, 19, 28–31, 91, 93, 170
  conflict-related risks 103–5, 107
  contracting researchers as risk 105–9, 159
  livelihoods/economic 3, 75, 93–7, 113
  psychological stress 97–8
  risks/risky environments 3, 11–13, 17, 22, 38, 44, 53–4, 86–7, 93–4, 96–7, 103–5, 109–12
  security problems 65, 94, 127–9, 158–9
  sexual harassment from contractors 128–9
  threats (death threats) 3, 9, 22, 93, 96, 101, 104–6, 108, 110–12, 159, 170
  unstable income 15, 22, 48–9, 93–4, 96–8, 159
interlocutors 9, 87, 108
intermediaries 9, 23, 34, 95
international journalists 41, 113. *See also* journalists
international NGOs (INGOs) 26, 36, 40–1, 135. *See also* non-governmental organizations (NGOs)
international organizations 32, 42, 98, 145–6
International Relations (IR) 10, 32
international research/researchers 8, 17, 26, 29, 39, 48, 70, 90, 100, 135, 138

Jharkhand, India 2, 17–18, 27, 43–7, 72–3, 78, 157
  Adivasis 17, 43, 45–6, 66, 71–3, 71 n.1, 81, 84, 109, 118–20, 122, 129, 131–2, 155
  bureaucratic hurdles and risky situations 65–8, 126–7
  local people/community
    broken promises of contractors 80–2, 131
    consequences for hosting researchers 111
    hospitality of 67–8, 81–2, 111
    misrepresentation of data 129–32, 165
    natural resources 17, 72

poor/unpaid remuneration 124–7
positive experiences of facilitators-contractors 153–6
sexual harassment from contractors 128–9
threats to personal safety 109–12
women's rights and empowerment 73–4, 118–20
journalists 7, 20, 27, 32, 41, 48, 113

Kujur, Aloka 73

Lakra, Barkha 73
The Lancet journal 169
language skills 9, 31, 44–5, 47, 51, 66, 69–70, 137–8
local assistants/researchers 7–8, 48, 66–7, 70, 75, 91–2, 131, 133, 136–7, 161, 171
long-distance approach 11, 148

marginalization 45, 77
Middleton, T. 13
Mind to Change organization 34
mission order documents (ordre de mission) 55, 58, 70
money 14–15. *See also* remuneration
multilateral development cooperation 47–8, 98, 146. *See also* bilateral development cooperation
mutual responsibility/dependency 13, 23, 40, 142–3, 147–8, 151, 158

national contracting researchers 23, 117–21, 123–4, 126, 128–9, 131–2, 137, 168. *See also* contracting researchers
Nature Medicine initiative 162
Naxalites/Naxalite movement in India 18, 66, 73, 73 n.2, 109–10

non-governmental organizations (NGOs) 18, 20, 28, 34, 36, 37, 40, 47–8, 61, 90, 92, 98, 133, 144. *See also* international NGOs (INGOs)
North-South knowledge production 3, 12, 41, 166, 175
economic inequalities 12–15, 161–2, 166
inequalities in 3–4, 22–3 (*see also* unequal relations in research process)

Office of National Security (ONS) 30

Parashar, Swati 5–6, 160, 174
part-time employment 37, 47. *See also* employment(s)
Patthalgari movement 18, 73, 73 n.3. *See also* Naxalites/Naxalite movement
Peace Corps volunteers 28
policy-oriented research 108
politics/political dynamics 31–2
power inequalities 3–4, 22, 118
power relations 45, 63, 83, 134
prejudice(s) 75, 119, 130, 132, 166

race/racism 7, 75, 118, 163–4
racial discrimination 41
remote research practices 11, 147–8, 155
remuneration (poor/unpaid) 3, 14–15, 17, 21, 24, 30, 35 n.2, 40, 44–6, 48–9, 51, 53, 57, 60, 71, 74, 91–2, 95–7, 123–7, 150, 158–9, 170, 173
additional costs 109
accommodation/communication/transportation 95, 100–1
at dangerous situations 98
data collection 102–3
medical expenses (illness/injuries during fieldwork) 98–9

broken promises by contractors 21, 72, 74–5, 77–9, 97, 113–16, 124–7, 159–60
research ethics 10, 15, 19–20, 118, 123, 136, 166, 170, 175
research facilitation 8, 16, 20, 26, 39
research funding 2, 4–6, 9, 13, 24, 41, 94–5, 102, 117, 120–2, 127, 132–6, 149, 162
  budgets 5, 40, 48, 60, 94–5, 103, 115, 128–9, 170–1
  unequal funding structure 4, 23, 132, 162, 167, 171
research institutions 11, 90, 118, 147, 162, 173
resistance movement 17–18, 72–3, 73 n.3. *See also Patthalgari movement*

Sanjek, R. 160–1
security/securitization 3, 10–13, 27–30, 38–40, 53–5, 57–8, 60–1, 91, 104, 147
  security problems 65–6, 103–5, 127–9 (*see also* insecurities of facilitating researchers)
Sida organization 40
Sierra Leone (research during civil war) 2, 5, 15–16, 18–23, 25, 25 n.1, 27–31, 43–4, 47, 49, 72–3, 117, 139, 157
  contract signing 30
  experience of facilitating researcher in 68–70
  Freetown 27, 37, 92, 138
  full-/part-time job for facilitating researchers 37–43
  importance of recognition 90–2
  less interest in involving local facilitators 135–8
  Ministries 30, 37, 136, 146
  non-recognition of facilitators 90–2
  post-conflict settings 3, 16, 27
  positive experiences of facilitator-contractor 139–42, 149–51
  assistance on building careers 143–5
  enhancement of status and opportunities 145–7
  long-term relationships 142–3
  remote research practices 147–8
  pre-war situation 28
  remuneration
    broken promises of contractors 113–16
    for facilitating researchers in 35 n.2
  research
    with privileged contracting researcher 35–6, 40–1
    with war-affected persons 34–5
  research funding 135–6
  security situation 28–9
Silent Voices blog 10
social mobility 32, 43
social science research 75, 165, 168, 170
sub-contracts 7, 9–10, 30, 95
Swedish Council 162
Syrian refugee research industry 14
systematic silencing of facilitating researchers. *See specific themes*

theory-data hierarchy 169
Toppo, Anju Oseema Maria 4–5, 9, 16, 18–19, 21
trust 23, 29, 52–3, 56, 82, 104, 142–3, 147–8, 150–1, 156

UK 16, 32, 142, 144, 146, 162
unequal relations in research process 2–4, 6–7, 11, 19, 22–3, 118, 161, 175
  contractors-facilitators relations (*see* contracting researchers; facilitating researchers)

economic inequalities 13–15, 161–2, 166
knowledge production 3, 7
unequal funding structure 4, 23, 132, 162, 167, 171
unethical authorship 24, 75, 77, 82, 112, 114, 120–4, 126, 163, 165, 168, 172
UNICEF 115–16
union-like organizations 173
The United Nations (UN) 20, 27, 37, 40, 45, 47, 98, 135, 159
The United States 11, 32, 59–60, 62, 121, 132–3, 146, 162–3
Utas, Mats 5–6, 33, 160, 175

Vancouver protocol 168, 168 n.2
Verweijen, Judith 5 n.1
Vincent, James B. M. 4–5, 9, 19
violence 3, 17, 58, 65, 76, 93, 99, 103, 108–9, 111, 130, 159

visiting researchers 43–4, 66–8, 80, 129. *See also* contracting researchers

West Africa senior school certificate examination (WASSCE) 34
white people, perceptions on 39–41, 69
women in facilitating research 16–18, 44, 61, 73, 76, 119–20, 125–6
  sexual harassment from contractors 128–9
workshops with facilitating researchers 5, 7–8, 15, 19, 30–6, 69–70, 73, 85–6, 92–3, 96, 109, 135, 139–40. *See also specific countries*
World Bank group 40, 135
World Vision International organization 40

Milton Keynes UK
Ingram Content Group UK Ltd.
UKHW021931091223
434008UK00003B/29